The Crafty Art of OPERA

for those who make it, love it or hate it

The Crafty Art of OPERA

for those who make it, love it or hate it

MICHAEL HAMPE

Translated by Chris Walton

THE BOYDELL PRESS

Translated from Michael Hampe *Opernschule. Für Liebhaber, Macher und Verächter des Musiktheaters*
First published in 2015 by Böhlau Verlag

First published 2016
The Boydell Press, Woodbridge

ISBN 978 1 78327 097 2

The Boydell Press is an imprint of Boydell & Brewer Ltd
PO Box 9, Woodbridge, Suffolk IP12 3DF, UK
and of Boydell & Brewer Inc.
668 Mt Hope Avenue, Rochester, NY 14620–2731, USA
website: www.boydellandbrewer.com

A catalogue record for this book is available from the British Library

This publication is printed on acid-free paper

Designed and typeset in Scala Pro and Scala Sans Pro by David Roberts, Pershore, Worcestershire

For my students

> 'That's why, as a man in need,
> If I'm to teach you the rules
> You should explain them to me anew.'
>
> Hans Sachs in *The Mastersingers of Nuremberg*

Contents

Note on the English edition

The English title for the book has been inspired by Alan Ayckbourn's *The Crafty Art of Playmaking*, published by Faber & Faber in 2004.

Michael Hampe and The Boydell Press (2016)

Acknowledgements

All illustrations are by Mauro Pagano (1951–1988) for productions by Michael Hampe and are in the author's copyright.

Preface

Do you love opera?

I love it and hate it.

You hate it? And yet you ...?

I love the genre, the works, the possibility of depicting the world through music.

But I hate the institution – the opera business that's supposed to bring these works to life in the manner they deserve. Instead, it's been treating them badly – albeit with some notable exceptions – for over four centuries. Regrettably, we use the same name for both the works and the institution: opera.

But you've been running opera houses and festivals yourself for decades!

Out of opposition! I wanted to change the institution. Sometimes I succeeded – for a short time, when the conditions were right. But then the natural inertia of the institution overpowered everything again. In brief: I have won battles, but lost the war. Opera cannot be changed.

So why this book?

The works don't stop asking for answers. Perhaps this book can prompt opera the institution to take a more serious approach to opera itself.

Il ritorno d'Ulisse in patria, Claudio Monteverdi/Hans Werner Henze, Salzburg Festival 1985

(top) Design for the Salzburg Felsenreitschule
(bottom) Detail of technical drawing

What is opera?

'What is opera?'

The question was posed to participants of a master class, all of them young opera singers. Their answer: silence. Only after some encouragement did they hesitantly proffer a few suggestions. One of them said: 'Connecting words and music'. Another: 'Grand emotions, publicly performed'. A third (he'd probably been reading about Wagner) ventured: 'The *Gesamtkunstwerk*' ('The total work of art'). The right answer – actually the simple answer – didn't come.

'Favola per musica' or 'dramma per musica' was the name of this new art form when it was invented some 400 years ago in Florence. And this expresses exactly what opera is. Telling a story through music – no, not 'telling': *enacting* it! A plot expressed through music. Music is opera's principal means of expression, as is the playwright's text in a play. In ballet it's the rhythmic motions of the body, and in film it's the moving images (hence 'movie'). In opera, *music* is thus a function of the action. It serves to express it.

Some might already be raising their eyebrows at this. 'Music *serves*? Doesn't he know that music *reigns* in opera?' We're not that far yet. 'Prima la musica – poi le parole' ('First the music – then the words'). This centuries-old dispute is pointless. Both music and words are dependent on the story, the action that initiates them. One could well imagine an 'improvisation-opera' in which the story is set out with just a few words – like in the *commedia dell'arte* – and all participants enact the story through improvised music. I once had a rehearsal pianist who was a gifted pedagogue, and when the singers' acting was awkward, he didn't play what was in the score, but instead improvised music, mimicking their affected behaviour. The ensuing laughter in itself answered the question about the relationship between music and the stage action. Or consider silent movies. The pianist would sit in front of the cinema screen and improvise music to match the images. When Rudolph

Valentino advanced towards Lillian Gish, the pianist would ascend in slow, chromatic modulations, climaxing in a harmonically sultry tremolo – the kiss – followed by a harsh *sforzato* – the slap Lillian planted on the cheek of the all-too-keen Rudolph. In both cases – our imagined, improvised opera and the silent movie – the music *serves*. In the second case it even serves a different art form, namely the cinema, thereby intensifying its effect.

It is only through the *score* that opera reaches its full heights. Once there is a score, however, music reigns sovereign and absolute. Everything has to conform to the score. Everything has to be configured and invented according to it; everything has to remain related to the music that's fixed in it. Only through this can opera find its justification. Otherwise one wouldn't need opera at all. Things could then be better expressed in other art forms. So opera music isn't 'just' music, it's music for a *purpose*. The difference between 'just' music and music for a purpose is often rather unclear, though it's easy to explain. 

in Beethoven's Fifth Symphony means: 

and nothing more. It's absolute music. It's abstract, though charged with great emotion. It is the musical material that Beethoven uses to construct the magnificent first movement of his symphony.

'Zu Hilfe, zu Hilfe, sonst bin ich verloren, der listigen Schlange zu Opfer erkoren' sings Tamino at the beginning of *The Magic Flute* ('Oh help me, oh help me, or else I'm lost, a victim of the cruel serpent'). He is accompanied by a hustling, chasing, pulsating music with a snake-like, rising motion in the bass. This is something totally different. Here, music has something very concrete to express and depict – namely, the specific panic felt by this specific Prince Tamino in a specific situation and in a specific state of mind. Music – the most abstract of the arts – is married to the dramatic art in order to express something very concrete. Music is being used for a purpose. Purists might even say: abused.

The difference between 'just' music and music for a purpose is not always clear in opera – sometimes even in its most venerable echelons. Some people think they are making music, whereas in reality they're making music for a purpose. And even critics are often unclear about it. They judge an opera on musical, aesthetic or historical criteria, which are all well and good, but the crucial yardstick is rarely mentioned, namely the truthfulness of the music on the stage and, accordingly, its usefulness. Critics often write of 'duplicating the music on stage', as if operatic music existed independently and wasn't instigated by the plot.

Speaking of 'usefulness' means asking: *what does the music actually say?* The composer Peter Cornelius once recalled an incident with Wagner at the dress rehearsal for the world première of his *Meistersinger*, when after weeks of rehearsals the entire work was running uninterrupted for the first time. Wagner suddenly cried out in exasperation – in his original Saxon dialect – 'Nu singen die Kerls wieder!' ('Now these fellows are singing again!'). All those present were astonished – for what else were the singers supposed to do? Wagner, though, had realized that the singers had lapsed back into their bad habit of just producing beautiful sounds, instead of expressing the reasons behind the sounds. In other words, they were again only making music instead of using their singing to elucidate the purpose of the music.

So what does the music actually say? How do we find this out? To achieve this, all the participants – singers, directors and even conductors – have to become 'music detectives'. What does a music detective do? The same as a police detective. The police detective stands before the dead body of a man killed with a knife. But the knife has disappeared. Then the detective finds a drop of blood on the ground, then another and another, near the exit. From these clues he deduces that the murderer carried the knife, dripping with blood, out of the door, and thus draws conclusions about the event as a whole. The music detective does just the same thing. There's a change of instrumentation – the clarinet enters, or there's a harmonic modulation or a dynamic shift, then a change in tempo. These, so to speak, are the music detective's drops of blood. They enable him to draw conclusions about the precise course of events that the music wants to express in a particular situation. In this way, he detects the reality behind the creation of the music that prompted the composer to write it this way and no other. To sum up: the composer makes the action sound as it looks in his imagination. The music detective (here the stage director) takes the opposite path and makes it look as it sounds. When both meet, the result is operatic bliss.

In this context, another question arises: *what* is the orchestra? When posed to the aforementioned young opera singers, the answer is again silence. At most there's a vague murmur. Someone says: 'The orchestra's simply there and plays.' Yes, that's what it does, without a doubt. But what *is* it? Finally, I offer my own answer: 'The orchestra is you! The orchestra expresses what's happening in the figures on stage – their character, their situation, their state of mind, their actions and reactions and many other things. *You* are the orchestra! That's why you, the singer, have to know the orchestra and understand what's happening in it.'

Of course the orchestra is a lot more than that, too. The orchestra can comment on what's happening, it can create an atmosphere, and when it plays leitmotifs it can create relationships and meaning. Besides offering the subjective expression of the performer, it can also provide an objective, external perspective. It can even play against the action – such as a triumphal march in which the victims of the triumph are paraded before us. However, the primary, most important function of the orchestra remains to depict the characters on stage in all possible aspects. Conversely, this means that they have to act in accordance with the orchestra.

But if the orchestra expresses what is happening to the singer on the stage, then the singer must turn the tables and appear as if *he* is creating the music. He has to provide the orchestra with the reason for playing this way or that. He first has to get excited before the orchestra can play his excitement. If the singer doesn't do this – or does it too late – then the orchestra has no reason for its excitement. The singer therefore always has to be a little ahead of the music. This, incidentally, is also how it is in everyday life. Before saying something one has to do two things: to think and to breathe.

One can understand and appraise the music in opera only in its relationship to the action on stage. In the spoken theatre, this apparent spontaneity is perfectly normal. Hamlet speaks his famous monologue 'To be or not to be' as if these words were occurring to him in that very moment, given the situation of his character. Only when this is the case will the audience think: 'Yes, he's good, we believe him', even though everyone knows that the words were actually written by Shakespeare 400 years ago. The same applies to the opera singer. We want to be able to believe him.

And what makes us believe him? What allows the audience to identify with the events on stage? How are they able to empathize, cry and laugh with the performer? In opera, it's always said that this is thanks to the singer's voice. Yet, strictly speaking, it's not the voice but the *sound* of the voice that counts. When a violinist plays Beethoven's Violin Concerto we are not interested in his fiddle, but in the sound that the player creates on his instrument, merging Beethoven's great soul with his own. It's the same with the singer. The voice is his instrument. It's the actual sound of his voice that touches people and awakens their interest in the character he is portraying on stage.

And what *is* this 'sound' of a voice? How is it created? Here is my definition: 'air + idea = sound'. The singer releases air from his body and this air is transformed into a tone by his vocal cords. This tone then encounters the 'idea', namely imagination: being sad or happy, angry or in love. A sad voice sounds completely different from a happy one, and everybody hears immediately whether someone is in love or aggressive. So it is the breath, transformed into a tone, which meets imagination, thus creating the vocal sound. And with this we are at the centre point of all theatre: imagination.

Theatre is founded on imagination. Without imagination, everything on stage is dead. The good news is: imagination can be trained just like the biceps. And a trained imagination will immediately turn everything into a vivid image. The basic element of theatre is a reality created by imagination, under the law of the 'Magic If' – *'if it were like that …'*. This is where imagination comes in. Every child has it. A piece of wood becomes a spaceship in which the child can navigate the universe. In the next moment, the spaceship can turn into a light sabre when its owner imagines himself a Jedi knight in *Star Wars*; and then the piece of wood changes again into a sailing ship when the child becomes a pirate of the Caribbean. His mother's call remains unheard because the child is so immersed in the reality created by his imagination. This talent for creating a reality from imagination is the fundamental prerequisite for all performing arts, regardless of the genre.

There can be two reasons for someone crying out: 'There's a mouse!' He can see a real mouse, which sends a message through his optic nerve into his brain, where mice are compared to lions. He might laugh at the harmless little creature; the stock comic figure of the old maid, on the other hand, would panic and jump on a chair. The other possibility is creating the mouse in the imagination. But this imaginary mouse, too, is still channelled through synapses into the part of the brain that compares mice with lions. And from here everything else happens as with the real mouse. There is just one condition for this: a specific area in our consciousness has to be dulled so that our brain does not cry out: 'There is no mouse!', but instead – like the child – accepts the fantasy mouse as real. It is precisely this kind of imagination that is at the heart of all dramatic talent. Strictly speaking, there is no difference between life and theatre. Both take place in a reality that determines our behaviour. This is why the great stage magician Max Reinhardt could with complete justification claim that: 'Nicht Verstellung ist die Aufgabe des Schauspielers, sondern Enthüllung' ('It's not dissimulation that's the task of the actor, but revelation').

Mind you, opera singers are not actors, nor should they be. They are music-actors. The difference between them is clear. The actor of Hamlet can speak his monologue slowly and pensively: 'To be or not to be ...'. But he can also laugh cynically: '... *that is the question!'* He is free to compose his own 'melody', so to speak. The music-actor is not free; he is bound to the score. But he can also come across as believable and authentic only if he lets the music emerge from a reality created by his imagination.

So it is imagination that controls, via the breath, both the sound of the voice and the expression of the body. Some indigenous peoples have only one word for both 'breath' and 'soul'. Perfectly plausible, since without breath there is no soul, and without soul there is no more breath. The means of conveyance of the soul – since it is *this* that is ultimately transferred from the performer to the audience – is the breath that controls body and voice alike.

The body was in fact the first instrument. In evolutionary terms, it existed millions of years before there was a voice. Even the ichthyosaurus could express itself unmistakeably through its body. Only much later did the voice emerge. But from then on they belonged together. Both of them together form the unity of vocal sound and bodily expression, controlled by the breath – or, if one prefers, by the soul. If things run as they should, one ought to be able to develop a kind of 'movement score' just as sophisticated as the music score and connecting with it, so that the two become one with the aim of embodying music. Wagner called this 'ersichtliche Taten der Musik' ('visible deeds of music').

These are, in brief, the basic elements of opera. Little thought is given to them, and their consequences are rarely drawn, let alone put into practice. Opera is unconscious of itself. So it is hardly surprising that, unlike all other performing arts, it has failed to develop a proper craft for enacting music during the 400 years of its existence. There is no canon of rules and techniques that must be learnt and mastered before being able to practise the art of opera. This makes it different from ballet, which demands many years of physical training, or film, which requires the skilful handling of a camera. Japanese Kabuki players practise for many years before they are even allowed to go on stage – not to mention Chinese opera with its artistic and acrobatic miracles.

Opera has developed just such a technical canon for singing, but not for enacting music. And singing is not acting. As a result, a young singer does his vocal exercises a hundred thousand times – perhaps even half a million times – before he becomes a singer. But he does not practise any pattern of musical movement, not even three times. Not because he doesn't want to, but because no one has ever told him that this is just as necessary as his vocal training if he is to achieve the desired unity of body and voice.

So in opera we are faced with the bizarre situation that scrupulous attention is paid to the musical value of every sixteenth note, but the scenic aspects are treated utterly arbitrarily in a wasteland without any rules. Anything goes! If someone announces loudly that he doesn't know any operas, that he can't read a note of music, that he's in fact quite unmusical and doesn't even *like* music – then it's pretty certain he will find one or more theatre managers declaring him a man of 'ground-breaking, thought-provoking, new ideas' and urging him to direct an opera. A medical faculty might as well commission me to carry out open-heart surgery, with all the media invited, to make it just the kind of 'event' that attracts attention. In both cases – the opera and my heart patient – the final diagnosis would run: 'operation successful; patient dead'. It is such absurdities that create the discrepancy, oft-lamented down the years, between the opera institution that naively renders homage to happy inadequacy, and the works of opera themselves that are at their best true marvels of humankind.

In defence of opera singers, it must be said that they often do much that is right. Some manage to develop their artistry of their own accord thanks to sheer talent and instinct, even under the most adverse circumstances. But the right way of doing things isn't taught. All is left instead to chance. The real deadly sin is: opera doesn't learn. To find proof of this, we only have to look at its history. From time to time there have been marvellous islands on which music theatre blossomed and achievements were made that should never have been allowed to slip away. Gluck and Wagner were such islands in operatic history, as were Mahler in Vienna and Felsenstein in Berlin. But the great ocean of amateurism washed them away every time. And afterwards, everything was just how it had been before.

Once more, the curse is: opera doesn't learn. This is why I asked myself: are there any rules and techniques at all that might serve as a basis for a canon of the craft of opera? In order to find this out, I and my students all over the world have systematically researched, rehearsed, tested and cross-checked many different notions – sometimes even by means of extreme, provocative experiments. To our surprise we found over a hundred techniques and rules that can be taught, learnt, practised and ultimately mastered and applied. To know them will be fruitful for everyone involved with opera – not just for those who make it, but also for those who love it, and even for those who hate it. We have therefore called them 'useful rules'.

Useful rules

★ Opera: enacting a story through music.

★ Understand the difference between music, and music for a purpose.

★ Define the purpose of the music.

★ Become a 'music detective'.

★ Know the orchestra.

★ Give the orchestra a reason to play.

★ Train your imagination.

Il ritorno d'Ulisse in patria, Claudio Monteverdi/Hans Werner Henze, Cologne Opera 1985, San Francisco Opera 1990

(above) Design for the in-house version

(left) Sketch of Tritons

The heart

How does theatre actually exert its impact? This happens on two different time levels: in the moment of performance, and in the memory. When I was a young actor, older colleagues of mine told me of their times spent working for Max Reinhardt in his legendary productions. Their memories were so powerful that they had tears in their eyes and could barely continue to speak. After more than half a century! Reinhardt had left a mark on them for the rest of their lives. I even suspect that time had intensified their emotional response, far beyond the original impression.

And am I any different? One of the most beautiful performances I have ever seen was Giorgio Strehler's production of Goldoni's *Le baruffe chiozzotte* (*Brawling in Chioggia*). I vividly remember the end of it – the reconciliation among the poor fishermen after all the commotion and the quarrels, illuminated by the light of simple lanterns while night descends over the autumnal, misty-grey Adriatic; and then there was the Cogitore, representing Goldoni himself as a junior lawyer, dressed in a wine-red coat (the only colour in the otherwise grey image), slowly drawing the curtain on it all. And when I describe it, I too am overwhelmed again and again by the sheer emotional power of the performance, even though it now lies almost fifty years in the past.

The fact that I came to opera was also thanks to such an experience. I was still in acting school and was auditioning in Berlin for a well-known theatre intendant (that's a title in Germany given to the administrative/artistic manager of a theatre or opera house). Obviously I wasn't too bad, because his assistant said he had two free tickets for an opera that same evening and asked if I would join him. Opera – what a dreadful thought! For a would-be actor to be interested in opera was something totally unfitting. But I wanted to be hired, so I said yes. And then, to my surprise, after a long opera performance I found myself breathless, with my heart pounding, right on the edge of my seat in the stalls. That was the moment when the suspicion arose in me that Mozart, Wagner and Verdi weren't the idiots, but *me*. I had confused the institution of opera with its works. Incidentally, the performance in question was the opening night of Walter Felsenstein's production of *The Tales of Hoffmann* that attained worldwide fame. Later, I had the happy opportunity to repay my debt to Offenbach and Felsenstein with a successful production of my own of the same opera, in commemoration of the hundredth anniversary of the composer's death, with Placido Domingo in the title role.

The intense impact of such moments is not as rare as one might think, and they happen in both performance and rehearsal. There are passages of such direct emotional power that even seasoned hands on the stage or in the auditorium are regularly overcome. These moments include Leonore's call to hope as the 'last star of the weary' and its searing horn introduction in *Fidelio*, Eva's outburst 'Oh Sachs, my friend' that untangles the knotted relationships in the *Meistersinger*, or the scene when the Count kneels before his wife with 'Contessa perdono' in *The Marriage of Figaro*. But it doesn't have to be these famous passages. No, even small, everyday happenings such as a glance or a gesture can touch our hearts directly. In such moments the great communion of theatre takes place: our heart recognizes the truth and needs no further proof.

So there it is, the be-all and end-all: the truth of the heart. Strictly speaking, all theatre knows only this one goal. How to achieve it isn't something that can be taught. All those involved – the author, the performers, the audience – can only find it together in their own hearts.

Thus it is that the most important rule of all can't be taught. But without it, none of those that follow is of any value.

Useful rule

★ Go straight to the heart.

Agrippina, George Frideric Handel,
Schwetzingen Festival 1985,
Cologne Opera 1985

(left) Sketch of Nero
(below) Technical drawing for set design

The seven 'W's

A young singer comes to his stagecraft lesson. He's a well-built, good-looking bass with a splendid voice.

'What do you want to work on?'

–'King Philipp's aria from *Don Carlos.*'

'Oho! Reaching for the stars already. But fine, let's try it. Who are you?'

–'Me?'

'No, not you, the character you're supposed to be.'

–'Ah, him. A king.'

'That's right, a king. And where are you?'

–'In Spain?'

'Yes, of course, in Spain. And *when* is it?'

(Pause)

'Have you ever heard about his great rival? Elizabeth – the First, not the Second, *she's* still alive today.'

(Another pause)

'The Shakespearean one?'

(He brightens up)

–'Oh, yes, there was that film' (He means *Shakespeare in Love*)

'Well, whatever. But I'm not here to test your knowledge of history. I really want to know: where and when is the king singing this aria? In what place? At what time of day or night?'

–'I don't know.'

'He's in his study or his bedroom. And as far as the time is concerned, it's mentioned in the text you're singing. The first rays of morning are entering through the window.'

–'Ah yes, that's right, I sing that.'

'So there we are. And now perhaps you understand the long introduction and you can draw conclusions from it about the state of the king, and what he does.'

–'What introduction?'

'Well, at the beginning the cellos sink into a persistent brooding, then there's the slow, circling motion that jumps up an octave, doubling the tempo, and almost drives him mad – it's the dreadful suspicion that's torturing him: 'Ella giammai m'amò'. Who is 'Ella'?'

–'I haven't a clue. And the rehearsal pianist never played me any introduction. We've always started where I come in.'

'Ah. Well, "Ella" is the Queen, and what's keeping the King awake all night is the terrible suspicion that she is having an affair with his own son.'

If one overlooks this young man's scanty knowledge of history, one really can't reproach him. No one has ever told him what his future profession is all about. His singing teacher ought to have explained to him that he can perform an aria meaningfully only if he knows the context in which it is sung. The rehearsal pianist should have done more than just bash the notes into him – he should have explained their significance, and should have told him how the orchestra's musical expression relates to what he sings.

As an initial step, it's good for everyone involved here – the singer, the director and the conductor – to ask the six basic 'W' questions: **W**ho? **W**here? **W**hen? **W**hat? ho**W**? **W**hy? In other words: Who am I? Where am I? (which also includes: where am I coming from, where am I going to?), When am I? What am I doing or want to do? hoW am I doing this, or want to do it? and above all: Why am I doing it? This does not yet describe the character in full, but it offers a kind of profiling, just like when the police is hunting for a criminal it hasn't yet identified. Using this basic information, our 'music detective' can begin his work.

And straightaway, an additional question arises with a seventh 'W': **W**hom is the character addressing? To whom is he speaking? Every form of living expression, whether uttered by man or beast, is addressed to someone or something. People speak to each other, to themselves, to God or to an animal – or even to an object or to an idea of someone or something. Every prayer is directed to a higher being; every struggle, be it mental or physical, is with an opponent; every love is directed at a person or an object. With 'To be or not to be', Hamlet ponders his suicide, speaking to himself; Xerxes sings Handel's famous 'Largo' (a beloved voluntary among church organists and really a *larghetto* aria) to his beloved tree. Many a servant, who never would dare to criticize his master in reality, addresses him in his imagination to tell him the unvarnished truth. The French call this 'L'esprit de l'escalier' – when one summons up the courage to speak one's mind only when already departing down the staircase.

When the addressee is imaginary, then it's advisable for the performer to make him more real by directly addressing one of the green emergency exit lights in the upper circle. 'Cruda sorte, Amor tiranno' ('cruel fate, tyrannical cupid') – green light (Isabella in *L'italiana in Algeri*). 'Komm, Hoffnung, lass den letzten Stern der Müden nicht erbleichen' ('Come, hope, let not the last star of the weary fade') – green light (Leonore in *Fidelio*). 'Se vuol ballare il signor contino' ('If the Count feels like dancing with me') – *no*, no green light here, instead Figaro is singing to the door that leads to the Count's chambers (as he has just explained).

It's no different when it comes to the animal kingdom. The threatening, snarling dog wants to warn the intruder, while the crocodile skips this part and goes straight to devouring his addressee. It's only through this counterpart, the addressee, that all expression comes alive. Therefore it cannot be said often enough: there is no expression without an addressee!

There are two exceptions, however. First: the insane. They truly seem to speak, eerily, into nothingness. Or at least they switch their addressee without any discernible reason. In his *Magic Flute*, Mozart offers us a well-nigh clinical study of a mentally disturbed person, in the scene where the three boys thwart the suicide attempt of Pamina, who is being driven mad by unhappiness in love. She constantly switches addressee abruptly. She speaks to her dagger as her bridegroom, caressing it in an erotic, near-obscene fashion: 'Soon, soon we'll be married.' Then it's the three boys whom she tells she wants to die. She displays the dagger to them as a very real instrument of suicide. Immediately afterwards, the addressee is a vision of her mother, the Queen of the Night, cursing her, and in the next moment she turns to the 'false young man', Tamino – all the while in stuttering syncopations, without any firm harmonic or melodic basis, until at the end, suddenly clear and determined, she decides to act. Now she sings in a firm, dotted rhythm: 'This iron shall kill me.'

According to this scene by Mozart, even the insane have someone or something to address, so they're not really an exception to the general rule after all. They are frightening because their minds are literally in dis-order. They switch addressee constantly without any obvious reason, making it difficult to recognize to whom or to what they are speaking. This then leaves just one, lamentable exception to the general rule that every expression has an addressee: bad opera! This unnatural phenomenon, regrettably, can be observed in many opera performances around the globe.

Useful rules

- ★ Start with the six 'W's: **W**ho? **W**here? **W**hen? **W**hat? ho**W**? **W**hy?
- ★ Then define the seventh: **W**hom? – the addressee.
- ★ Locate the addressee.
- ★ Change the addressee where necessary.
- ★ If the addressee is imaginary, choose a fixed point and address it instead.

Agrippina, George Frideric Handel, Schwetzingen Festival 1985, Cologne Opera 1985

(left) Sketch of Agrippina

(below) The finished costume

Sense and sensuality

More than any other art form, opera addresses our senses. This is both its strength and its weakness.

> Ihr wisst, auf unsern deutschen Bühnen
> Probiert ein jeder, was er mag;
> Drum schonet mir an diesem Tag
> Prospekte nicht und nicht Maschinen.
> Gebraucht das gross, und kleine Himmelslicht,
> Die Sterne dürfet ihr verschwenden;
> An Wasser, Feuer, Felsenwänden,
> An Tier und Vögeln fehlt es nicht.
> So schreitet in dem engen Bretterhaus
> Den ganzen Kreis der Schöpfung aus.
>
> As you know, on our German stages
> Everyone tries out what suits him.
> So don't hold back today
> With backdrops or machines.
> Use the heaven's greater and lesser lights,
> And let's have plenty of stars,
> Water, fire and rocky crags,
> Animals and birds.
> Let the whole round of Creation
> Tread out these narrow boards.
>
> (Goethe, *Faust I*, Prologue on the stage)

Opera doesn't need to be told this. It addresses our emotions and our intellect, along with all our senses. Its rhythms possess our physical body, our pulse races, our nerves tingle, our blood pressure rises, pain disappears, and all while our eyes and ears revel in beautiful images and sweet music.

In the heyday of opera, when the upper classes kept their own boxes at the opera house, culinary and erotic delights were also the order of the day. For example, there was the 'aria di sorbetto' – an aria sung by a less important character that didn't demand the listener's full attention, leaving him free to focus on supping his champagne and slurping his lemon sorbet. And once his thirst was quenched, he could close the curtains of his box in order to satisfy further appetites – opera no doubt played its part in keeping the birth rate healthy. The vestiges of that era could still be seen in the old Teatre del Liceu in Barcelona before it burnt down in 1994. The 'chambres-séparées' behind the boxes were all still there, with their dining tables and their curtains to provide the necessary privacy to the upper crust. Opera, as the Babylon the Great among the arts, always had a strong penchant for dissolute delights. The danger in all this is that opera's multifarious appeals to the senses means the *sense* of the whole undertaking gets lost. There is nothing better suited to lulling us into gentle slumber through sensual indulgence than the art of opera. When opera offers so many delights, why should one care about its actual content? 'Don't gawp so romantically' cursed Bertolt Brecht. It didn't help much.

And yet composers have expended much effort in making this content knowable through their music and in conveying the sense of it clearly, in the details as well as the overall context. To this very end they have spent centuries developing a gigantic, all-encompassing, constantly expanding musical arsenal: all for the purpose of conveying content and sense to their audiences. Because the audience needs sense. If it can't make sense of what it sees and hears, it cannot 'play along', and the result is dead theatre. However, before the audience can get involved, the sense and purpose of the music must be understood by those who are actually performing it.

Once, during a rehearsal of my production of *Così fan tutte* at the Salzburg Festival, it so happened that a grand old lady of opera – the legendary *Kammersängerin* – paid us a visit. Her world fame was founded on her unsurpassed interpretations of ladylike roles such as the Marschallin in Strauss's *Rosenkavalier*, the countesses in Mozart's *Figaro* and Strauss's *Capriccio*, and of course Fiordiligi in *Così fan tutte*. This great artist, now an exigent pedagogue and mentor, was greeted by all with due reverence when she emerged into the auditorium. She had come to appraise a student of hers in her debut as Fiordiligi.

The rehearsal took its course up to the scene in which Fiordiligi – hitherto of unwavering fidelity – at last succumbs to the seduction of the tenor Ferrando. She abandons her resistance to the accompaniment of the most ravishing oboe phrase in all opera, sighing: 'Fa di me quell che ti par' ('Do with me what you will'). The lovers sink into each other's arms, singing blissful chains of thirds. Fiordiligi – reluctant no longer – is tenderly drawn to the bed by Ferrando. She had donned the black military overcoat of her fiancé Guglielmo when she was planning to flee – but now he opens it to reveal her beautiful, naked shoulders and upper body, and gently lays her on the bed.

At this moment, Don Alfonso bursts out of the wardrobe where he has been listening with the betrayed Guglielmo. He swiftly draws the curtain across the scene while gazing out in embarrassment at the audience. He has won his bet that both sisters – Dorabella and Fiordiligi – can be seduced within twenty-four hours. But to be right is no longer amusing when it means ruining so much happiness of others. Our Alfonso, the wonderful José van Dam, played this in such an inimitable manner that it provoked long applause at every one of the performances.

At this rehearsal, however, there was no applause. Instead a verbal torrent of moral indignation emerged from the auditorium towards me. 'No, no, no! You can't do that! *Really*! To undress Fiordiligi and have her half naked on the bed. A little kiss, fine, perhaps! But not on the bed! Fiordiligi – this lilywhite blossom – no, no, no!'

I tried to pacify the indignant lady as well as I could by promising to change the scene (I was lying). All those around me looked as embarrassed as Don Alfonso. Was it possible that moral attitudes had changed so much over the course of just one generation? Or – one hardly dared to think it – had the most famous Fiordiligi of the century failed to comprehend the very sense of the work?

Useful rules

- ★ Find out: what does the work mean?
- ★ Consider: what does your role contribute to it?
- ★ Make sense. Both in the details and in the overall context.
- ★ Sense trumps effect.

Don Giovanni, Wolfgang Amadeus Mozart,
Salzburg Easter Festival and Salzburg Festival 1987

(top) Preliminary sketch
(bottom) Final set design for Act I

Bodies in space

Curtain up! The performer takes the stage. Straightaway a relationship exists between his body and the space in which he moves. Perhaps he's coming along the centre line from way upstage to the front as a mighty ruler, as a conqueror, or as blind Oedipus as he taps out his path with his broken sceptre. Or he's emerging swiftly from the wings as a servant, a conspirator, or a surprise guest. Or he appears backstage right, crossing the stage diagonally as a messenger or a man about to plead a suit before his sovereign. In all these cases, the relationship between his body and the space is already part and parcel of the events being depicted.

However, the performer's body does not just enter into a relationship with the stage space, but also with all the other bodies and objects that are in it. And thus a tiny universe is created that obeys the same laws as the universe itself with its orbiting planets and galaxies. This stage universe, too, knows attraction and repulsion, gravity and centrifugal forces, tension and release. And in the magical space of the stage, even supernova explosions can occur, as can black holes that swallow up everything. Even invisible dark matter can be felt in the 'aura' of a performer – something no one can define, but that draws everyone under its spell. This bodily phenomenon, however, has its own boundaries: in the spoken theatre, these boundaries are some 25 metres across, in the opera roughly 32 metres. And auditoriums should respect these boundaries, too. After all, you can't fall in love at a great distance, and this is precisely what should happen in the theatre: the audience has to fall in love with the performers. In opera, this little stage universe has yet another dimension: the music. Whoever wants to be a master of this small universe would do well to follow rules derived from those of the Big One. And indeed, such rules exist.

One overarching rule from which many more are derived, is: sameness is dull. Two bodies that stand before the audience in the same pose at the same stage level are boring (though this happens all the time). The dissimilar, however, is interesting. The character singing should stand further back in relation to the one listening; the latter could then stand with his back to the audience as he reacts to what he hears. This creates tension and counter-tension. It also has the advantage that the singer can project his voice forwards, he can see the conductor and can also address his partner. All the great painters do it like this – for example, when Rembrandt painted Christ on the cross, he placed Him in the light with the dark silhouette of a Roman soldier in the foreground. Goya depicts a proud beauty walking haughtily past a dark, stooping beggar-woman in the foreground. 'Dios la perdone. Y era su madre!' ('May God forgive her – it was her mother!'), he wrote under it.

Almost all singers are drawn as if by magic to the centre of the stage. How dull is that, with the right and left sides both the same! The centre stage is at best the place for a king, who cannot play himself, but depends on his royal courtiers bowing to him. Standing at the golden section is far more interesting (in proportions roughly one third to two-thirds), with the short tension on one side and the long tension on the other. Incidentally, this is usually the acoustically most advantageous spot. At La Scala Milan it's called the 'Callas point' because the great diva knew how best to dominate the space. At this spot, you almost automatically adopt a position at a slight angle to the stage ramp. This is far better than standing parallel to it – a position preferred by many that I call the 'pancake position'.

A symmetrical space tends to exude a kind of noble dullness. This is why it's regarded as anathema, a deadly sin, by those who are anyway suspicious of any strict form. But they forget that asymmetry can be created by the bodies in space, resulting in a high degree of tension between symmetry and asymmetry.

From time immemorial, the circle has been a magical figure. Two or more bodies standing in or on a circle exist in a strong relationship to each other, almost regardless of how they are placed.

A particularly high degree of tension can be created by means of the 'lion–tiger walk' – two performers circling each other like two stalking beasts, or like a binary star, bound one to the other through attraction and repulsion. Of course, it can well happen that one of them – in opera, it's usually the tenor – decides he doesn't give a hoot about all these lions and tigers and binary stars. So he turns to face the audience instead in order to offer them his brilliant high notes. All the tension that had been built up is promptly lost. Every time this happens it is as if one of the planets in our Solar System had decided to cease orbiting the sun and embarked instead on a stroll through space as a glittering comet. It wouldn't end well. And the same is the case with our tenor. If he were a boxer, he'd long be lying KO'ed on the floor. I've called this disastrous habit 'the tenor's turn'.

In life, it's usually very unpleasant to come under fire from two sides, whether it's a battalion on the field of war, a man torn between two jealous women, or Odysseus navigating Scylla and Charybdis. One rarely emerges unscathed from such a situation, so one tries to avoid it. On stage, however, this position can be dramatically enriching and effective. It should be sought out wherever possible. Even if it's only so one can act and react on two fronts. From ancient tragedy to French boulevard theatre, from Classical opera to the American Western, all dramatic arts utilize this constellation in order to heighten tension. A prototype of this is the scene in Goldoni's *Servant of Two Masters* in which Arlecchino has to serve a meal to both his masters at the same time. Giorgio Strehler's world-famous production drove this scene to the point of delirium while at the same time offering a brilliant lesson in how to produce dramatic sparks when you're placed between two fires.

It is also a curious phenomenon that one intuitively expects the leading voice in an ensemble to come from the left (though it is sometimes difficult to decide which voice is actually leading – see, for example, the famous quartet 'Mir ist so wunderbar' – 'How strange I feel' – in Beethoven's *Fidelio*). Perhaps it is only because the first violins in an orchestra also normally sit on the left. Or because the spectator's heart beats on that side. I've never been able to find a conclusive answer. Nevertheless: we feel comfortable when the soprano stands on the left and the bass on the right, and rather uncomfortable with the reverse of this. Naturally, one can also play with this expectation by turning everything around and on its head and then the right way round again – such as in Rossini's turbulent finales. We can observe the same phenomenon in the visual arts. Most Baroque painters placed the raised throne of a ruler to the left, with messengers, envoys, supplicants and defeated enemies approaching from the right.

In any case, a performer is well advised to leave enough air around him. If he comes too close to other performers or objects, he loses power and significance. Even a piece of furniture can involuntarily become a competitor – though one can also use this effect on purpose. The rule is: 'The King goes forth to France.' The right side of the stage is England, the left is France. The closer the English King gets to France – i.e. to the centre stage – the weaker he becomes. If he crosses the border, the French King can either receive him with honours or throw him in the dungeon. The English King would do well to stay in his own country and forcefully present his point of view (literally!) from there. And he should also avoid those little steps that many singers make, because they express nothing and only let him appear insecure. When he walks, he should do so with a specific goal and to a specific purpose.

The relationship between body and space has an extreme impact when there is violence or torture on stage. In the two-dimensional visual world of film and TV there are many scenes of extreme brutality. The observer might watch them reluctantly, but they are nonetheless bearable. It's different on stage: its three-dimensional corporeality soon makes violence to the human body unbearable to many. I have experienced it in several of my own productions. In one, the curtain had to fall on the turmoil. In another, several people would faint at every performance. On one occasion, my wife, sitting in the director's box, was even spat upon by an enraged member of the audience, although the torture on stage could not even be seen. It had only been announced, and preparations for it made. The rest had been provided by the audience's imagination, proving its worth as a marvellous 'co-performer' in creating a reality all of its own.

So now the stage space actually expands out into the much bigger auditorium – the large, cavernous space that needs to be captivated by the body and breath of the performer. Great Zen masters are said to have been able to hold an auditorium under their spell for a long time, simply by slowly increasing the tension of their breath and body. In opera this is facilitated by the music, which generates tension by means of its own predetermined melodic, harmonic and rhythmic relationships. Ideally, the auditorium should enclose the audience snugly and end where the last members of the audience are seated. Because every extra metre of space has to be filled by the tension of the performer's breath. He has to reach even those members of the audience seated in the very last row – and if he doesn't, the audience coughs. A sentence or a musical phrase therefore has to be held with full intensity right to its very end. It's like the arch of a bridge that has to reach the opposite shore, otherwise one falls into the water. In opera, the opposite shore is the last row of the topmost balcony, and the water is the orchestra pit. The bigger the auditorium, the more breath one needs. An experienced performer will use his breath to exert dominion over his fellow performers and his audience, like a charioteer commanding his horses. He can tighten the reins, steer to the left or the right, or suddenly give his horses their head and gallop off with them. Body and voice here form a unity, steered by the breath, in accordance with the laws of space and time. Over the course of my life in the theatre I have become convinced that music and the stage follow these laws no less than the atom or the most distant galaxies. They all play with attraction and repulsion, with gravity and centrifugal forces (whether intact or disrupted), with inhaling and exhaling: the great, eternally renewed play of tension and release. Whoever is able to command this, is a master.

Useful rules

- ★ The body in the space is already part of the action.
- ★ Develop a feeling for space in relation to your co-performers.
- ★ Sameness is boring. Be dissimilar.
- ★ The singer stands further upstage, the listener further downstage.
- ★ Position yourself according to the golden section, not in the centre.
- ★ A king can't play himself. Those surrounding him play him.
- ★ Stand at an angle to the stage ramp, not in the 'pancake position'.
- ★ Maintain your relationship with your partner. Avoid the 'tenor's turn'.
- ★ Seek a position between two fronts. It's dramatically effective.
- ★ Wherever possible, place the leading voice in an ensemble on the left.
- ★ Leave space around you. Otherwise objects can become competitors.
- ★ Hold your stance – don't wobble around.
- ★ When you move, make sure it's with a purpose and a specific goal.
- ★ Violence and torture have a greater impact on a live body on stage than in the two-dimensional images of film and TV.
- ★ Fill the space with breath. If the audience coughs, you've got too little breath.
- ★ Regard sentences and musical phrases as the arch of a bridge. Make sure to reach the other side.
- ★ Master the play of tension and release.

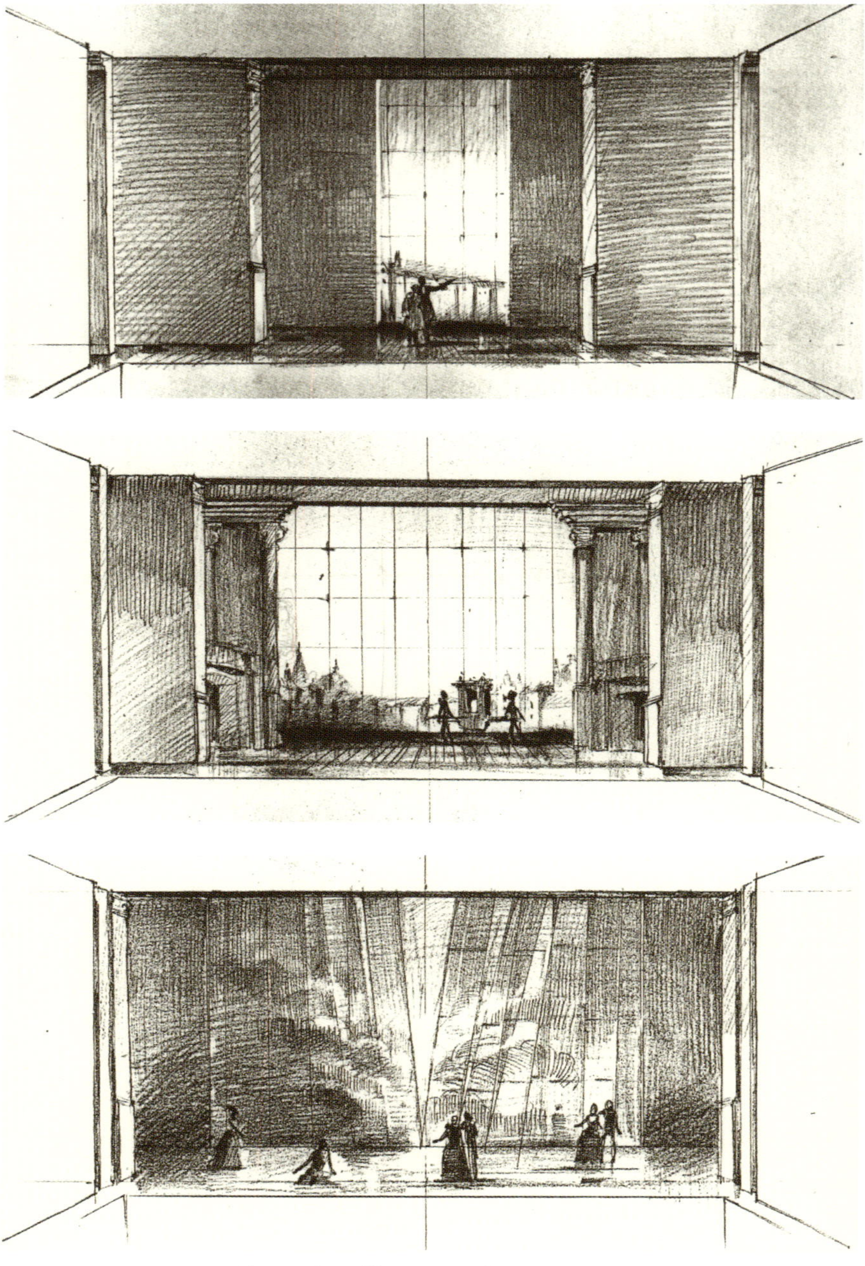

Don Giovanni, Wolfgang Amadeus Mozart,
Salzburg Easter Festival and Salzburg Festival 1987

Preliminary sketches

Movement

Who has ever seen a soul? Not even the devil in Goethe's *Faust* can grasp it:

> Und wenn ich Tag' und Stunden mich zerplage,
> Wann? Wie? Und wo? Das ist die leidige Frage.
>
> For hours and days I rack my brains,
> When? How? And where? – the puzzle remains.
>
> (Goethe: *Faust: Der Tragödie zweiter Teil,* Act 5, lines 11,630–1)

The soul can express itself only through the breath that animates both body and voice. And these are the two basic elements of opera. So it's all the more surprising that only one of these – the voice – is subjected to many years of strict training, while the other – the body – is completely neglected, even though it is by far the older instrument of the two. The un-trained, un-controlled body can play nasty tricks on the soul that yearns to express itself.

What actor or singer doesn't remember the agony endured during their studies when their body and voice refused to express what they felt so vividly inside? Regrettably, as far as the body is concerned, this state of affairs often remains the norm with opera singers for the rest of their career. That's because their body was never given the rigorous training it needs. Goodness knows how they can expect to express anything properly amidst all their straddle-legged pressing, their uncontrolled gesticulating and fidgeting, and their soul hiding in the most impossible places – their shoulders, elbows or knees.

If the soul is located anywhere, then it's in the solar plexus, at the centre of the gastric nervous system, our 'second brain' that in evolutionary terms is far older than the cerebrum and so functions far more unconsciously and animalistically. It refuses to obey the brain. The nervous singer about to go on stage can order his stomach 'Be calm' a hundred times, but it won't help, for the stomach does what *it* wants. It's at this 'life-point', the body's 'core', that feelings emerge and then move up into consciousness. Mozart composed this process superbly in the introduction to Donna Anna's recitative when she recognizes her father's murderer in *Don Giovanni*. This terrible awareness rises up from an unconscious, primeval source over the space of two bars until it explodes into consciousness: it is neurology and psychology expressed as one in music. Every language expresses this physical fact in a different way – in English, we speak of 'acting on gut feeling'; in German one 'makes decisions from the gut' ('aus dem Bauch entscheiden') or even 'feels it in one's urine' ('man spürt's im Urin'). It's through this animalistic, ancient bodily system that the soul sends out its signals.

So it's also here – in the centre of the body – that bodily movements have to find their origin. The great actor and director Fritz Kortner recommended observing animals for this. To watch a panther at full speed, the flight of an eagle, or a dolphin playing in the waves lets us understand what it means when physical movement begins organically at the centre. On stage, this natural process is linked to an artistic purpose. Kortner's obsession with expression could sometimes drive him to overdo things. For one particular production he needed dogs – dangerous dogs. His wish was a command to the theatre management, so a bunch of fearsome, snarling mastiffs was paraded before him. So fearsome that his actors were delighted to obey his instruction to go off for a break and leave him alone with the hounds. They became concerned when no word came back from him for a while. So a scout was sent to check that all was well. When he returned, he reported in horror that he'd seen Kortner kneeling in front of the beasts, ardently trying to get them to perform the expressive crescendo he desired, shouting 'No, not ruff-ruff, it's WUFF WUFF!'

In opera, the animalistic movement of the body must be united with the music. The breath has to bring voice and body into a unity. And there's the rub – indeed, it's one of the fundamental problems in opera. All too often, the body doesn't play along. The singer lacks the necessary control over his locomotor system, and his untrained body disavows his well-trained voice. Everyone has had to deal with this problem who has ever engaged with opera, be it on practical or theoretical terms. Training opera singers ought to pay the same attention to their body as it does to their voice. But this is not the case. Years of vocal exercises stand alongside meagre, unpopular movement lessons. Stanislavski's sequence of exercises: 'difficult – normal – easy – beautiful' has no hope of being realized under these circumstances.

For a long time – until the mid-nineteenth century – it was the ballet master who acted as the stage director and movement instructor in opera. This was not without good reason, because when it comes to moving musically, the same basic training is suitable for both opera and ballet. Only afterwards do the two genres diverge and become specialized in their own field. For as long as it is devoid of such a training in musical movement, opera will always be left to chance, dependent on the talent and instincts of individual performers. This is an unsatisfactory state of affairs because it means that one half of the operatic art remains unfulfilled. After all (with certain exceptions), the body is supposed to make visible and comprehensible what we hear with our ears. We can hear a violinist better if we can also see him.

The prerequisite for this is a plastic, unforced execution of movement and gestures. The audience has to be able to 'read' these, otherwise they are useless. One clear gesture, executed cleanly, is always better than five brief, hurried gestures. How a performer gestures and how he moves across the stage is generally allied to a specific goal, steering the audience's attention to the particular 'focal point'. One can even underlay such gestures with a text. For example, in order to avoid senseless twisting and waving when others are summoned, the underlaid text in rehearsal could be: 'You there, come here and look that way!' This simple 'baby text' technique makes the procedure itself clear and comprehensible.

Fidgeting and fumbling is usually the death of musical theatre. They destroy the impact of the singer who's doing the fumbling, the impact of his co-performers and above all the impact of the music itself. If a singer on stage hates a colleague and wants to distract from his or her performance (which happens occasionally), all he has to do is to pretend to catch flies while the other one is singing. There's nothing one can do about it if it happens – for the audience will have eyes only for the fly. Many productions in recent years seem to have raised this technique to the level of a general principle.

Fumbling can ruin the loveliest music, as we can see from the following example. We're in the first act of Strauss's *Der Rosenkavalier*, during the morning levée of the Marschallin. Everyone is listening to the aria of the Italian tenor. Rightly so, because the theatre management has spared no expense and engaged a superb tenor for this brief number. But at his first high notes, the audience becomes restless. The tenor notices this and exerts himself all the more. He sings ravishingly, but now there is laughter at every one of his top notes – and at the end, the audience whoops with delight. What had happened? The animal dealer was standing behind the tenor with the 'Hunderln, so klein, und schon zimmerrein' ('doggies, so small and already house-trained') demanded by the libretto – two Pekinese. No doubt prompted by some frequency inaudible to the human ear, one of them kept wagging its fuzzy tail enthusiastically at every high note, in time with the music. It was adorable, and the audience enjoyed the diversion to the full. At that moment no one had eyes or ears for opera, art or *bel canto* any more. And the tenor afterwards swore he would never again share the stage with an animal.

Little dogs and flies obey a very simple, basic principle: the eye spontaneously follows every movement it sees. That's why movement must be coordinated with the music. If it isn't, it destroys its impact. When I tried to explain this to a group of extras, their leader interrupted me: 'Just tell us straight out. Which would you prefer: "Stumme Jule" or "Spannemann"?' The man had grasped the essence of their task; 'stumme Jule' ('silent activities') means carrying out lots of little actions such as are found in a busy background crowd of people, while 'Spannemann' ('man agog') means listening intently with wide-open eyes and bated breath, as if at a showdown.

Naturally, it also often happens that a performer remains immobile and expressionless, leaving the orchestra to express the tempest raging inside him. Expression here is split between the body and the music. But the tension of the breath will remain always linked to the music. If this were not the case, one would be demanding something of the singer that he cannot do, because he has only one diaphragm, one source of breath, and one body with which he can express just one thing at a time (unlike the music). He can look only to the right or the left, but not both at the same time. What he *can* do is to alternate quickly between two states, two body postures, between fear and courage, sadness and joy, deeply felt emotion and irony. The performer can make full use of this possibility, and many scenes derive their impact from it. But to demand a descending gesture while the orchestra and the vocal lines are ascending would mean doing violence to the singer. If forced long enough to do this, he will withdraw into what he's learnt, namely just singing, and otherwise try to save his skin as best he can.

Since music on the other hand can express many different things at the same time, the principle of an ensemble becomes possible in which the voices and the orchestral accompaniment are divided between different people and have a life of their own. In this case it is all the more important that their physical, visible representation is kept in line with the score. Otherwise, we risk confusing the audience by offering them an uncoordinated chaos. One good example is the sixteen-part fugue in the fight scene of Wagner's *Meistersinger*, in which the cantus firmus of the old masters is maintained resolutely throughout, and is contrasted with the quarrels of the individual solo characters that emerge from the general battle of the various chorus groups, and disappear again into it. To make the complex musical structure of this fugue visible and comprehensible in the stage action, despite all the turmoil, could serve as a suitable test for upcoming music theatre directors.

Of course there are also numerous occasions when one has to act *against* the music. But even here, the movement of the performers still has to remain linked to the music, *ex contrario*, so to speak. To take our 'fly' example again – here, the fly would have to learn counterpoint. Executing such an action against the grain of the music demands a lot of skill. It has to be calculated very carefully so that it does not result in an unmusical chaos.

Just like the music, movements too begin with the 'upbeat' of the breathing impulse. Every forward movement begins with a slight movement backwards, and every ascending movement begins by reaching up from below. Thus there emerges a rhythm of tension and release that creates a sense of lightness and elegance. In this respect, opera singers should learn from circus artists. Without this precisely swinging rhythm, every juggler would miss a catch and every trapeze artist would land with broken bones in the circus arena. The traditional Chinese opera manages real miracles in this department. I once saw a performance in which the heroine, with four flags perched on her back, sang coloratura worthy of our Queen of the Night; while singing, she caught two lances thrown at her in the air and threw them back in the rhythm of the music, then repelled the next lance with the sole of her raised foot, still singing all the while. She ended her coloratura with a kung-fu triple salto, landing with her feet on the ground exactly in time with the final cymbal crash. With just a little of this artistry, how our opera would blossom!

In every activity in opera, it's important to unite the movement to the music so that we avoid unmusical gesticulation. This also applies to handling props. The danger of such unmusicality is particularly great when dressing or undressing – which is a common occurrence on stage. For example, Don Giovanni and Leporello have to swap clothes at the beginning of the second act of Mozart's *Don Giovanni* while Elvira is singing her long, yearning, melodious lines on her balcony in the rays of the dying sun. Any uncoordinated sartorial flourishes here can wholly destroy the magical A-major twilight mood of their trio. In such cases it's advisable to divide up the activities into different subsections, and then to tie each of them to the single phrases of the music.

One bad habit common to many performers (and many people in everyday life) is that of constantly leaning forward to give emphasis to what they are communicating. Such bowing is really appropriate in only two cases: among servants, and when a person loses control through anger or despair. Karl Lagerfeld once told me that tailcoats in the eighteenth century were cut precisely – 'épauler' – so as to prevent such bowing movements. People were supposed to have an aristocratic posture, and so their tailors ensured that they maintained their social attitude – in line with the old saying 'clothes make the man'. The whole social repertoire of bodily movement, from the emperor down to the beggar, is one of the most important physical means of expression. So it has to be mastered.

The same is true when it comes to postures depicting different states of mind. Happiness takes wing, unhappiness weighs us down. Our body and its movements are light and buoyant in the first instance, but very heavy in the second because we are 'de-pressed' (the word says it all). A cry, on the other hand, always goes upwards to the heavens, be it in triumph or pain. Even when a torturer presses us down, our body reaches upwards as we cry out. And if a bullet hits, knocking our body down, our death cry still reaches out and upwards as we fall. If someone wants something, he holds out his hands, insisting on what he wants. But on stage, people usually give up too soon, without driving the tension to its logical extreme. The same is true of all types of conflict, be they mental or physical. Duels are focused through the eyes, just as are hate or love.

Opera's use of the language of music means it expresses great emotions. Accordingly, it's often accused of being pathos-laden with its exaggerated, 'operatic' gestures. This is both true and untrue. A tenor's top C that's properly supported by his diaphragm will automatically demand a certain expansiveness of gesture. And above all: pathos does exist – in life itself and even more in opera, in which all expression is magnified by its reliance on music. The despairing Medea does not kill her children without pathos. The rule is simple: the emotion must be greater than the gesture. If the gesture is bigger than the emotion, then it's indeed 'operatic', too laden with false pathos. The depth of emotion must correspond to the volume of breath. Big feeling demands big breath.

In opera, it would be ideal if a 'movement score' could be derived from the music. Just as singers acquire a vocal technique in order to perform the musical score, so too could they acquire a physical technique with which to compose their 'movement score' during rehearsals. If one were to combine both these 'scores' and unite them into one, the result would be the unity of voice and movement, both animated by the breath of the performer.

Useful rules

★ No soul without a body.

★ Bodily expression precedes speech and music through the 'upbeat' of the breath.

★ Movement starts at the centre, the solar plexus.

★ Emotions rise up from the solar plexus to consciousness.

★ 'Act from your guts'.

★ Observe the movements of animals and learn from them.

★ Train your body as a musical instrument, just as you train your voice.

★ The order of practising is: difficult – normal – easy – beautiful (Stanislavski).

★ Gestures must be plastic and readable, otherwise they are useless.

★ One clear, cleanly executed gesture is better than five small, quick ones.

★ Underlay gestures with 'baby text' in order to make them more readable.

★ Direct gestures towards the focal point.

★ Fumbling is the death of both theatre and music.

★ The eye spontaneously follows movement.

★ Determine when to split musical and physical expression.

★ The body can do only one thing at a time; music can do many things.

- The body and the breath can oscillate rapidly between different states of being.
- In ensembles, individual movement must be coordinated with the music.
- When actions and movements go against the music, make sure they are in counterpoint with it.
- Movements begin with an 'upbeat' in the opposite direction.
- Find the rhythm of movements like circus artists.
- Link activities to the music. Sectionalize actions and match them with single musical phrases.
- Don't bow forwards unless you're a servant or when you lose control.
- 'Épauler' – hold your bearing.
- Happiness takes wing, unhappiness weighs down.
- A cry always goes upwards.
- Be insistent; don't give up too soon.
- Duels are focused through the eyes.
- Don't be afraid of pathos. But the emotion must be bigger than the gesture.
- Big feeling demands big breath.
- Create a 'movement score' that matches the musical score.

Don Giovanni, Wolfgang Amadeus Mozart,
Salzburg Easter Festival and Salzburg Festival 1987

(top) Set design for Finale I
(bottom) Sketches of Donna Elvira, Donna Anna and Don Ottavio

Le physique du rôle

Having the right body for a role is vitally important, as is knowing how to move it. This is called: 'le physique du rôle'. I'm almost tempted to regard this as the most important aspect, even more important than the voice. Because the body was the first and earliest instrument of expression. When casting a role, both aspects should be treated at least equally, also with regard to the other roles involved. It's not just the voices that have to fit together, it's their bodies too. Only under this condition can opera attain fulfilment. When this is *not* the case, hopes of success are stymied from the outset. However beautiful the singing, and however honest the efforts of everyone involved – not least the costume designer – one will always come up against the original defect. And one will always end up dissatisfied. Many opera houses pay far too little attention to this aspect when casting roles. It's not just a big mistake: it's one of the main reasons for the widespread dissatisfaction with opera.

Different languages also produce different attitudes and patterns of movement. One can observe it when children play. Without the slightest knowledge of languages, they use gibberish and mimicry to ape a gangling, gum-chewing American, a wildly gesticulating Italian, a rigid German or a blasé Frenchman. And in opera, too, the cast should be chosen in such a way that the language employed emerges idiomatically and credibly from the physical behaviour and social status of the character.

At this point it can be profitable to consider the world of cartoons. Mickey Mouse and Co. often apply the principles of opera far more consistently than opera does itself. Cartoons offer a perfect transformation of music into physical expression. Of course, cartoon characters can be drawn by hand or in the computer according to the needs of the music. Or, conversely, one can compose the music according to the cartoon characters. This is easier than embarking upon a tiresome search for a real living person able to create movement and music in a single action. And yet opera can learn a lot from cartoons. If roles have been cast with the right vocal and physical characters, the mechanical effect of cartoons can even be recreated on stage. The following episode can prove it.

For many of his productions, Karajan used to make a studio recording of the music before rehearsals had even begun. This was also the case for our production of *Don Giovanni* at the Salzburg Easter Festival. And he required his recording of the music numbers to be played at the scenic rehearsals. I didn't like this, because the singers should create the musical expression themselves on stage. But he insisted. And since the same singers were on stage as had sung in the recording, the final rehearsals in their costumes, with their masks and the right lighting, produced a fascinating effect. Even those actually participating in the production were unable to tell whether a singer was actually singing, or whether his voice was just coming from the loudspeakers. And so it happened that in the scene in which the quartet of servants invites the peasants to attend the ball in the castle ('Su, svegliatevi; da bravi! Su! coraggio, o buona gente' – 'Come, wake up everyone! Come, courage, good people'), Karajan interrupted: 'Gentlemen, you're rushing. Once again please!' Everyone looked on sheepishly, and began again. And again Karajan interrupted, now visibly irritated. 'No, no! In time! You're racing ahead!' I screwed up my courage and said softly to him: 'But this is your recording.' 'Really?' he asked, and his eyes narrowed briefly. And then, unmoved: 'Once again please!' And after it was done, triumphantly: 'There you go! Why not do it like this right away?'

This episode teaches two things. First: that playback opera is indeed possible. When the silent singers offer the right physical interpretation, a mechanically reproduced music can prove astonishingly effective. Some productions of musicals today use this effect and are very successful at it. Many opera lovers might be horrified at the notion of this separation between the voice and the body. But today's technology makes it possible, and such methods may be useful for certain aspects of musical narrative, or for pedagogical programmes.

But this divergence of stage action and recorded music also demonstrates the crucial limits of all things mechanical. Machines might be practical, they can save money and time and achieve great effects. But one has to know where and when to use them. For they have no breath, no upbeat and thus no soul. They don't really belong in the theatre. Only what can be filled with breath, or makes use of breath, belongs there. One could create great theatre with three naked people in the desert – as long as they are gifted with imagination. One who wants something, another who wants the opposite, and a third who will judge the case – be it as chorus, policeman, or the audience. In essence, this is all that's needed. Without these three people and their imagination, even the most wondrous, technologically up-to-date opera house is useless. Theatre can only be made by a human body that is animated by breath and moved by imagination. This hasn't changed since the very beginning. And herein lie both the limits and the uniqueness of theatre.

Useful rules

- ★ 'Le physique du rôle' is a decisive criterion.
- ★ Study and utilize the physical gestures of different languages.
- ★ Give a character the gestures of his or her social status.
- ★ Study good cartoons.
- ★ Only what has breath and an upbeat belongs in music theatre.

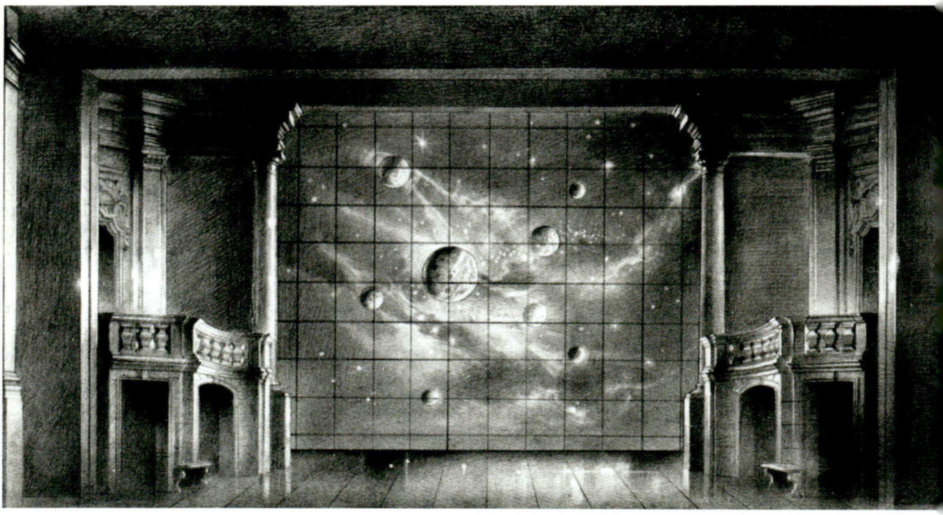

Don Giovanni, Wolfgang Amadeus Mozart, Salzburg Easter Festival and Salzburg Festival 198

(top) Set design for Finale II

(bottom) Drawing of the universe for projection and plastic planets for the last act

Discomfort and inconvenience

Rembrandt wanted to paint a picture: 'Joseph tells Jacob his dream.' It was intended to be a big painting, which meant its composition had to be well thought-out. So Rembrandt prepared for it by making several sketches.

The first shows Jacob sitting comfortably, with little Benjamin between his knees, listening to Joseph as he stands before him telling him his dream. It promised to be a beautiful painting. Everyone would immediately understand what it was about. But Rembrandt wasn't content. The second sketch shows Jacob sitting once again, and again with Benjamin between his legs; but now Joseph is standing to the right, so that Jacob has to turn away from Benjamin to listen to him. It's less comfortable, but for this very reason it makes what Joseph is saying seem all the more important. So it was better – but still not interesting enough for Rembrandt. The third version shows Jacob seated, but with his back half-turned to Joseph, and Benjamin is no longer between his knees but is leaning against his left side while Joseph stands to the right. Now Jacob has to twist himself away from Benjamin in order to devote his attention to Joseph. It looks very uncomfortable as he sits with half-open mouth, listening to what his son has to say. This makes the figure of Jacob highly expressive and intensifies our interest in Joseph as well, because one doesn't accept this degree of discomfort if what is said isn't of great importance.

The comfortable is the enemy of expression – or, to put it another way: the greater the discomfort, the more intense the expression. And discomfort isn't just about bodily posture. In spatial terms, it is also possible to position yourself in a way that's either comfortable or uncomfortable. A miscreant answering to an inquisitor behind him – thus out of his sight – will certainly not regard his position as comfortable. The same is true when a conflict takes place among people in pouring rain, or in a boat being tossed about by waves.

Of course discomfort has its boundaries, especially with opera singers whose primary task is to sing beautifully. Even when they are in an uncomfortable position, their diaphragm and breath still have to be relaxed and fully under control. If this is not the case, their breath support is impaired and so is their singing. But – within what is technically possible – the general rule is that the uncomfortable is better than the comfortable because it is more expressive.

Allied to this is the technique of incorporating obstacles in a scene. I observed this in the work of the aforementioned Fritz Kortner. Nothing could satisfy his obsession with expression. After a long, exhausting rehearsal, a scene finally seemed to work. But he was still not satisfied, grumbling: 'It's all going too easily, too smoothly. I need obstacles.' The actors cast their eyes to the heavens. My god, they were all half dead, and on top of everything else he now wanted obstacles. He noticed their reaction and said: 'Ah, you're rolling your eyes and thinking the old man's lost the plot. But he's not crazy. You just don't know that obstacles create expression.'

Only much later did I understand just how right he was. In general, people don't want to show their inner feelings. They try to hide them. But an obstacle can bring them out into the open for others to see. An obstacle can even intensify expression in banal, everyday actions. For example, if someone looks outside through a door and bends to the side in order to see something hidden by the doorpost, this intensifies his expression. It also makes the object he's observing seem more interesting. The obstacle – the doorpost – makes the observer more expressive. Now he wants to exit through the door, but a chair stands in his way. So he sinks down into the chair in despair because he's just lost a million. Or he kicks it angrily into the corner, furious at the fraudster who's cheated him of the money. But if the whole thing turns out to be a mistake and he's won a million instead – why, then he jumps for joy over the chair. Each time, the chair – the obstacle in his way – prompts him to a greater degree of expression than he would otherwise have shown.

Props can be wonderfully stubborn obstacles. If you have to do something quickly, but instead get entangled in the coat you're trying to put on, this can create a torrent of expression. And the old slapstick trick of having to manage three or more objects with just two hands has brought forth famous comic and tragic scenes.

Obstacles enrich and intensify expression. They increase the tension and make people and things more interesting.

Useful rules

- ★ The comfortable is the enemy of expression. The uncomfortable is more expressive.
- ★ Incorporate obstacles in a performance. They increase tension and interest.
- ★ Use props as obstacles.
- ★ Develop slapstick scenes (where appropriate), using obstacles.

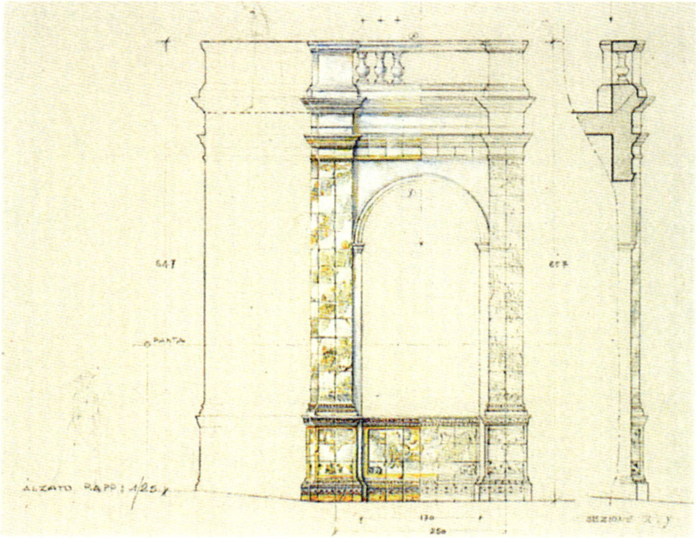

Così fan tutte, Wolfgang Amadeus Mozart, Salzburg Festival 1982, La Scala Milan 1983

(top) Set design for Act I
(bottom) Detail of technical drawing

Bank robbers

Opera singers have generally not robbed a bank. Thank God for that! On the other hand, had they done so, they would have learnt how all kinds of shady figures behave – conspirators, murderers, terrorists and, of course, bank robbers too. Such dodgy characters can be found in many operas. They act inconspicuously when planning their dirty deeds; they meet as if casually, in the shadows on the walls, not out in the open; they speak softly, with seeming indifference and immobile expression; and their eyes are always scanning the scene for possible dangers. Once they're about to crack open the bank safe, bank robbers reduce their words and gestures to what's absolutely necessary. They act slowly and carefully, avoiding all hasty, accentuated movements that could trigger the alarm. All this happens under the greatest possible tension and with bated breath.

There are plenty of such scenes in the operatic literature, but many opera singers play them freely, insouciantly – as if they were the owners of the bank. They simply refuse to acknowledge the robbers' true state of mind and ignore the ominous tension in the orchestral accompaniment. They just have no experience of such things. So a healthy dose of bank robber's imagination could really help.

In such hazardous moments when discovery threatens, the tension can even be heightened by little mishaps – such as a tool clattering to the floor. Or when Pedrillo is organizing the escape in Mozart's *Entführung aus dem Serail* and has to manage the necessary ladder through the narrow, squeaky metal gate; or when Romeo is climbing up to Juliet's balcony and nearly loses his grip, about to fall. In such scenes, the audience has to root for the character, holding its breath in anticipation. But they'll do this only if the character himself plays his part under great tension.

Just about every opera also has someone in a hiding place, spying on others. They too have to demonstrate the tension of their situation – the danger of being discovered, the exertion involved in eavesdropping so they can catch every word. Even if their hiding place is constructed so they can't possibly be seen by the others, allowing them to relax while eavesdropping, without fear of discovery, the audience will find their being hidden believable only if they play it with the right tension, with pounding heart and bated breath. This is one of the many peculiar phenomena of theatre.

Speaking or singing 'asides' also belongs to this category: when a character says something to himself or to the audience that the person standing next to him mustn't hear. This is naturally completely unbelievable – why should a thousand people sitting on the other side of the orchestra pit be able to hear something that his partner on stage can't? This ought only to work if there is a wall between them – but this is never the case except for Pyramus and Thisbe in Shakespeare's *A Midsummer Night's Dream*.

So what can be done? There are two techniques one can use to make an 'aside' at least seem plausible. The first is to build a metaphorical 'wall' by turning aside, seeking cover behind one's own shoulder. 'You are the noblest and the best' oozes the smarmy servant to his master, but then turns away and adds scornfully over his shoulder: 'What a scoundrel!' The quick shift in body posture and in the tension of the breath suggest plausibility.

The second technique is to give 'cover' to an aside by doing something. The person speaking the aside might tie a shoelace or open a bottle; or the addressee might utter a flattered laugh and turn away with a wave of the hand, thereby providing the necessary cover for the other's aside. Both techniques can also be combined up to a point where no one finds anything odd about the aside (which is also often a punchline). Of course speaking an aside is a convention, an agreement between performer and audience, as so much else in opera. But conventions also need to be filled with life and made credible.

Useful rules

- ★ Conspirators act under tension, but inconspicuously.
- ★ Prepare your evil deed with few slow movements and with bated breath.
- ★ Mishaps can increase the tension.
- ★ When in a hiding place, play out the tension of listening and the danger of discovery – otherwise the audience won't believe you're in hiding.
- ★ Speak 'asides' behind the 'wall' of your own shoulder and/or combined with an action.

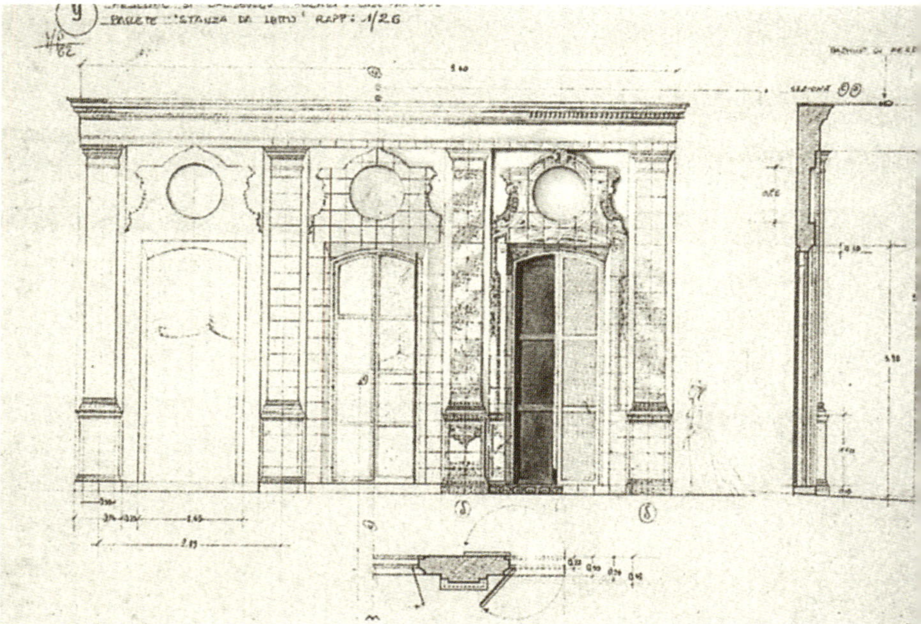

Così fan tutte, Wolfgang Amadeus Mozart, Salzburg Festival 1982, La Scala Milan 1983

(top) Set design for the sisters' boudoir *(bottom)* Detail of technical drawing

Pretend theatre

'As soon as the roaring trombone sounds, go this way' says the Priest to Tamino and Papageno during their trials in Mozart's *Magic Flute*. To underscore his command, his right hand points somewhere up in the air, while his left hand holds a burning torch. Tamino and Papageno would have to fly in order to follow his instructions. Instead of simply pointing to the (clearly visible) dark passage awaiting them, the Priest pretends that he is showing the way. No idea of space or intent directs his gesture. And this happens not only with small gestures but also with great emotions. The singer pretends that he loves or hates, but without actually feeling either emotion. One can experience it all the time: the orchestra in turmoil, the vocal line at fever pitch of passion – and yet something's missing, namely the actual emotional and physical state of being, the breath of big emotion that alone could make all this believable. The singer's body betrays him – especially his hands, which are telling us: 'It's not really that bad. There's no reason for the orchestra to get so worked up.' There is no reality created by imagination whatsoever. The singer offers merely 'pretend' theatre.

This refusal to depict a character's true physical and mental state is one of the capital problems in opera. It's one of the reasons opera can seem awkward and ridiculous. But perhaps singers do this instinctively with good reason. Because singing (and making music in general) is a far more technical activity than acting. The famous violinist Yehudi Menuhin once said: 'Expression is the enemy of technique.' In opera, this means that the more a singer immerses himself in the condition of the figure he is portraying, the more he runs the risk of neglecting his vocal technique. This is why it is so important that singers should learn to unite the voice and the body during their training, both of which must be controlled by the breath demanded by the emotional and physical situation. If their character sees a monster, their physical expression of horror has to provide their diaphragm with the necessary support for the high note and the *sforzato* that give musical expression to their horror. In such cases, sometimes a compromise is necessary between the condition they must express and the technique they need to use. A Medea, raising her arms to heaven to curse herself and the world, might have to declare that she can't and mustn't stretch her arms all the way, because then her larynx would also ride upwards. This would make it impossible for her to project her curse above the fortissimo of the orchestra. I always suspected that this was one of the reasons why the great sorceress of expression, Maria Callas, lost her voice so early. She was so superbly expressive and submerged herself so much in the mental and physical state of her characters that she neglected her technique as a result.

My own encounter with Callas was an unhappy one. On her last tour, she and the tenor Giuseppe Di Stefano came to the Mannheim National Theatre where I was working as a young intendant. She wasn't doing herself any favours with this 'final tour'. Her voice was gone, and it was painful to experience how this great artist reduced herself to singing innocuous pieces, such as Puccini's 'O mio babbino caro' from *Gianni Schicchi*, which didn't tax her voice. Word had somehow spread that she was about to arrive at the theatre, so there was quite a large crowd gathered at the stage entrance. She got out of her limousine, dressed elegantly in black, just as one knew her from countless photos. She also wore a large, striking hat. I greeted her with due deference and accompanied her to the stage. She then informed us where she and the tenor would enter and stand during the concert. She also expressed her wishes regarding the lighting in a perfectly professional manner: the main light from the side at a specific angle, and only the necessary minimum from the front. In order to help the effect, I whispered to the lighting technician: 'And use a soft light to make her beautiful – add amber and rose to it.' She heard me, though I had assumed she didn't understand German. After a pause, she gave me a long, sad look, then in a melancholy voice, just like the Marschallin in *Rosenkavalier*, she merely said: 'Ja, ja'. I wished the ground would swallow me up. I'm still ashamed today about my inadvertence, however well meant it was.

When Callas assumed a role, she came close to fulfilling what the great opera reformer Walter Felsenstein used to demand – namely that singers had to enter into their role to such an emotional extent that there was nothing left for them beyond language, except to sing. I found this dubious because it seemed to replace imagination with pumped-up, hysterical emotion. It reminded me of the anecdote about Laurence Olivier and Dustin Hoffman (as told by Hoffman himself). Hoffman had to portray his character in a dishevelled, exhausted state, and so he stayed up for three days and nights without shaving or washing in order to embody the part. At which Olivier reputedly asked him: 'My dear boy, why don't you try acting?'

There is another danger here: in their endeavour to enter into the physical and emotional state of their character, many singers mistake forcing for intensity. So they not only force their voice (which doesn't do the voice any good) but also cramp their body. You see them jerking forwards and downwards at every musical accent, rather like a turkey picking at corn. This is forcing! Intensity, on the other hand, is always breath. In our everyday lives too, our pulse races when we experience strong emotion, making us take bigger breaths. A big emotion always demands big breath – and this is the opposite of forcing. The voice rests on the exhaled breath, which causes the body to stretch backwards like the recoil of a gun. This is intensity!

The great moments in opera are derived from their emotional intensity – their breadth and depth of feeling. We find this intensity in the great operatic works. That is what makes them just as alive today as when they were written, and carries them over the centuries. Herein lies the principal difference between Mozart and Salieri, or Wagner and Meyerbeer. Whereas a normal, healthy person measures 37 degrees Celsius in his heart, the heart of the great composers sometimes beats at 370 degrees. And they require this blazing, fiery intensity from their poor interpreters, too. This is what makes it so difficult to do justice to the great masterpieces of opera. They demand that we pay for it with our own emotions, with our own humanity. 'Pretend' theatre won't help. The path from doing to being, which is the aim of all theatre, is a thorny path that few have traversed all the way to its end.

Useful rules

- ★ Don't pretend to do or feel something. Just do or feel it.
- ★ Merge expression and technique into the unity of body and voice.
- ★ Don't mistake forcing for intensity.
- ★ Imagination is better than hysteria to reach a high emotional level.
- ★ Sing on the breath, not on your vocal cords.

Così fan tutte, Wolfgang Amadeus Mozart, Salzburg Festival 1982, La Scala Milan 1983

(top) Set design for the garden, Act II

(bottom) Detail of technical drawing for the ship with the red sail

The 'trizophrenic' upbeat

As mentioned already above, we all have to do two things before saying anything: thinking and breathing. Only then is speech possible. This is even truer of music. The expansion of time in an arching musical melody demands the appropriate breath, plus the corresponding emotional span. Therefore it is eminently necessary to be 'ahead' of the music. Only then can the singer seem as if he himself is creating the music in that very moment; only then can his voice and body form a unity. While the singer is singing one phrase he must already be preparing himself inwardly for the next so as to connect it to the first. And, above all, he has to use the upbeat of his breath to make the orchestra his servant, his vehicle of expression, in order to explain to the audience the meaning of the music emerging from the pit. It happens all too often that singers breathe when they already should be singing, while the orchestra stampedes away without any visible reason. This is a sure sign that the singer did not think – more generally, he did not 'switch' on time. Lagging behind the music like this, instead of 'creating' it in good time, can often be involuntarily comic.

The decisive element is the upbeat. Anyone watching me teach might be irritated by my frequent interjection: '*And* – ' just when the singer is singing at his most beautiful. His concentration on the sheer beauty of his sound makes him forget the upbeat to what's coming next. In my childhood we had an old housekeeper who had the habit of ending her sentences with '*and* –'. As in: 'I'm going shopping now, *and* –'. The effect was magical because the whole family would be waiting to hear what came next. It was the magic of the upbeat. '*And* –' is the magic formula for all types of upbeats. Long ones drawn out over several bars, and short ones; hard, soft, exalted or graceful upbeats. Upbeats for every type of music and movement. This is because body and breath are always involved, and the musical sorcerer's apprentice would do well to practise his upbeats over and again until they become second nature. One can do this in everyday activities such as putting on a pair of trousers. '*And*' pick up trousers, '*and*' open them, '*and*' right leg, '*and*' left leg, '*and*' pull up, '*and*' button '*and*' zip. Yes, it's banal, but this is how events on stage are turned into a fluid musical continuum. The upbeat breath of having an idea awakens the interest of one's fellow performers and makes the audience curious. 'What's he up to now?' is their reaction.

To be sure, there are also occasions when the upbeat mustn't be made visible. 'Don't phone your opponent ahead', said an old judo master to me once. 'Otherwise he'll know what you're planning. You have to surprise him.' That is true in many situations, for instance in so-called 'false exits': 'I'm going, and you'll never see me again! – but there's just *one* more thing...' Many a singer will give us the impression that although he's announcing his exit, he isn't really going to leave. He's 'phoning ahead'.

A sure sign of the quality of a performer is his 'switching speed' – in other words, how quickly he can move from one thing to the next. One expression must follow the next clearly – *secco*, drily, rather like a sausage slicer will cut off one slice of salami after another. This 'speed' should be considered carefully when casting certain roles, especially in Mozart. But even when switching fast from one thing to the next, the upbeats still have to be placed clearly, with two contradictory things borne in mind. On the one hand: the strength of a slap to the face depends on how big a swing you take. On the other hand, don't 'phone ahead'. That requires a delicate balance for all upbeats between spontaneity and control, depending on the situation at hand. During one of our rehearsals, Herbert von Karajan once raised his baton to begin, but straightaway put it down again, saying 'Too loud', even before anyone had played a note.

When it came to giving upbeats and being prepared in advance, musicians and singers alike could feel completely secure with Karajan. One always knew well in advance what he was going to do next. I wanted to find out how he managed to do this, so during a break in rehearsals I finally asked him. 'I don't know', he muttered, 'I do my yoga every morning.' I wasn't going to let him off the hook, so I became insistent: 'But you're conducting one thing, yet inwardly you're already doing another one. That's kind of schizophrenic.' 'No', he answered, 'trizophrenic' (that isn't a word, but he used it anyway). 'Trizophrenic! I give a cue and straightaway I have to signal to the horn that it's too loud, and at the same time I'm already preparing for the next tempo change. You might say: the cue to begin is the present, the horn is already the past and the tempo change is the future.' And indeed, all musicians have to operate on these three levels, especially opera singers. One can't learn it from one day to the next. It needs a lot of practice. Karajan's 'trizophrenia' creates what I call the 'flow of life' in a musical performance, where one thing emerges organically out of another.

Useful rules

- ★ Be ahead of the music and 'switch' in good time.
- ★ Lagging behind the music is unintentionally comic.
- ★ '*And* – !' is the magic formula for the upbeat, for both the music and the action on stage.
- ★ Decide which is the more important: either 'don't phone ahead', or 'take a big swing to slap hard'.
- ★ Train Karajan's 'trizophrenia': cue, control and preparation, all at the same time.

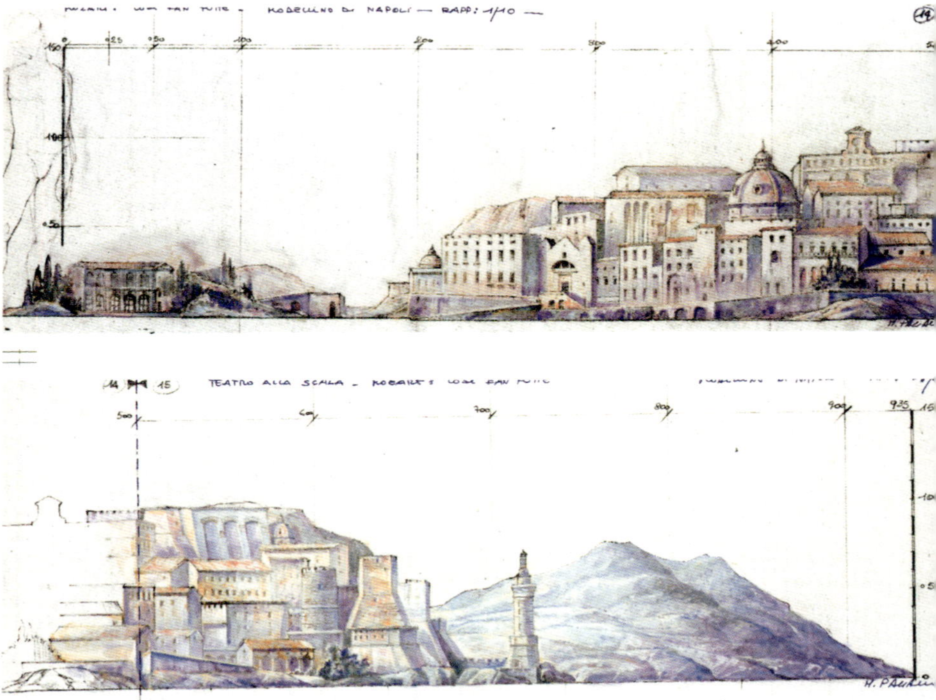

Così fan tutte, Wolfgang Amadeus Mozart, Salzburg Festival 1982, La Scala Milan 1983
Technical drawing for the plastic model of Naples

The complete music-actor

I'd been warned: he would sing the role of Falstaff the same way he always did, and not give a damn about the production. He arrived along with his charming wife Tilda, then spent two uncommunicative days observing suspiciously what we young upstarts were up to. Then Tilda passed judgement: 'Tito, tutto questo sarà un' amore. Fai tutto quello che vuole' ('Tito, this will be a love affair. Do everything he asks of you'). 'He' – that was me, the director. From this moment onwards, Tito Gobbi – the most famous Falstaff of his era – rehearsed the role with us as if he were singing it for the first time. Everyone was deeply impressed by his artistry: he didn't think it beneath himself to engage with ideas from younger people, while at the same time he was teaching them a lot himself. Tilda turned out to be right – this production became his last great triumph.

Tito Gobbi was the complete music-actor. No one was more in control of his craft, and he was able to apply it to tremendous effect. When he sang the role of Scarpia (usually alongside Maria Callas), his opening words 'Un tal baccano in chiesa!' ('What an uproar in church!') exuded such a glacial iciness that every audience froze to the spot. And when he appeared as Falstaff at Herne's Oak in Windsor Forest, replete with stag's horns in his disguise as the Wild Hunter, everyone in the audience held their breath. The way he sang and acted out Verdi's twelve strokes of midnight with their shifting harmonies was spookily magical.

Gobbi was capable of elementary fits of rage – both in character and in private. One of our performances was taken over by a guest conductor who annoyed Gobbi throughout the evening. In the forest scene, Falstaff holds Alice in his arms underneath Herne's Oak, but she slips out of his grasp and he cries out, exasperated: 'Il diavolo non vuol, ch'io sia dannato!' ('The devil doesn't want me to be damned'), followed by a wild orchestral eruption. But on this occasion, Gobbi turned to the conductor he now so despised, and declared – completely in his role: 'Il diavolo ben vuol, che TU sii dannato!' ('The devil would love YOU to be damned!'). The poor conductor got such a fright he almost dropped his baton.

Even when the orchestra was playing fortissimo, every word that Gobbi sang could still be understood. 'Masticare le parole' ('Chew the words') was his motto. And this he did, over and over until everything came out crystal clear. Each syllable then took its natural place in the musical and rhythmic structure with a perfect balance between vowels and consonants. But he insisted that this was nothing compared to what Laurence Olivier did, whom he had befriended in London. Olivier had confided to him that he recited every sentence exactly 110 times before going on stage to play one of his big Shakespearean roles.

Gobbi had a further method for making sure his diction was comprehensible: 'In every sentence, pick out the two most important words ['due parole'] that the audience *has* to grasp in order to make sense of the whole. Regardless of the circumstances, it's these words that one has to get across clearly, so that even those in the very last row can hear them.' In Baroque opera that was simple, he maintained, for the text was simply repeated so often until even the dullest in the audience got it. But where this isn't the case, said Gobbi, one has to rely on the 'due parole' and on 'masticare'. The latter without the music if necessary – but with a cork from a wine bottle clenched between one's teeth until the text has been fully mastered. With Gobbi, the result was an articulation that was clearer and more comprehensible than I had ever heard.

Regrettably, this art of articulation has been almost lost today. Either because singers often don't really understand the language they're singing and assume the audience won't understand it either, or because of surtitles ('They can read, can't they?'). This is a dreadful loss for the unity of words and music, each of which finds its meaning only in the other. If the text can't be understood, then the music can't be understood either.

Another technique that Tito Gobbi taught me was this: 'Come tu metti i piedi è il ruolo' ('How you place your feet is your role').

How right he was! One can try it out oneself by imagining a peasant or a sailor walking with a straddling, rolling gait, and then contrasting it with the refined leg posture of a prince looking down on the world. Or a Beckmesser in Wagner's *Meistersinger*, who might walk like a stork, and mark out Stolzing's singing mistakes as if spearing them with his pointed beak. The singer's feet connect him with the floor and determine his overall posture. How many tenors trying to be fiery lovers come across as unintentionally comical because they stand with legs wide apart, forcing out their notes. No one has taught them any better, and they didn't have the good fortune to learn from Gobbi.

In Gobbi, a complete mastery of his craft was at the service of a stupendous imagination. This combination enabled him to portray a character on stage down to the smallest nuance, and to do so wholly in the context of the music. One could learn much, very much indeed, from Tito Gobbi.

Useful rules

- ★ 'Masticare le parole' – chew the words until they are completely comprehensible.
- ★ Practice your lines out loud, with a cork clenched between your teeth.
- ★ Look for the two words in a sentence that are vital for its meaning. Make sure they are understood by everyone in the auditorium.
- ★ Your role is how you place your feet.

Così fan tutte, Wolfgang Amadeus Mozart, Salzburg Festival 1982, La Scala Milan 1983
Set design for the opening and closing scenes

Mozart

'A lot was stolen from Mozart', said an audience member to Richard Strauss after a *Rosenkavalier* performance. Unmoved, Strauss replied: 'Well, do you know anyone better?' And indeed, Mozart is the best teacher in opera. One can learn everything from him. Above all, one cannot cheat with him. If a singer chooses Mozart for an audition, his strengths and weaknesses will be obvious after just a few bars. Murphy's Law applies all too well in Mozart: what can go wrong, often will. Stylistically, he's hard to characterize. Often, what he does is little different from his contemporaries, and yet he constantly turns convention into revolution. However brilliant new ideas and concepts might be, they won't help with Mozart. All one has to do is already in the score. All elements for a good performance can be found in it. 'It's simple, but simple is difficult' (Goethe). Mozart's simplicity is the most difficult of all. Only stagecraft and integrity can help here. 'The heart ennobles the man' is the best-known quote from his letters.

Whole libraries can be filled with what has been written about Mozart. It seems that everything has already been said. But in fact, little has been said about what 'opera-makers' can learn from him. And the lessons Mozart can teach are well-nigh inexhaustible. Here's a few of them.

In Mozart, a lot of things happen very quickly – in comparison to other composers, many more things happen in Mozart at any given time. His rapid shifts in musical expression and his abrupt emotional changes demand an extremely fast, inner 'switching speed' in order to anticipate the next phrase that already has different music. 'Mozart is a brain problem' said John Pritchard, my longstanding music director at Cologne Opera, who was famous for his interpretations of Mozart.

For many performers, this speed is too much to handle. They can't keep up with Mozart, so they try to salvage the situation by resorting to a one-fits-all expression that ignores the ever-changing differentiation of his music. And in fact, he does demand a lot. Sometimes his musical structure changes every two bars – even every bar in some cases. In the first quintet of *The Magic Flute*, the Three Ladies describe the effect of the magic flute: 'Der Traurige wird freudig sein, den Hagestolz nimmt Liebe ein' ('He who is sad will become joyful; the old, misogynist bachelor will be overcome by love'). These are seven bars *alla breve*, each one of them with its own expressive content. In the first, the bassoon hangs its head sadly; in the second the violins offer a kind of 'abra-cadabra!' so that in the third bar, the sad man skips merrily away. In the fourth, the horns and violins unite for a brief flourish as if to say: 'Aren't you amazed', moving without any transition in the fifth bar into a kind of gastritic staccato characterizing the old misogynist, who in the sixth bar is overwhelmed by emotion from the cornucopia of violins, from which in the seventh love flows into his heart with the bright sound of the oboe. And because the three Ladies aren't just describing this but are themselves in love with the 'beautiful youngster' Tamino, Mozart puts the cherry on the top by adding a flirty grace note on the word 'love'. The micro-management necessary for the music of such passages demands a lot. One mustn't overdo it either; but ahead of every one of these bars one has to 'switch' inwardly from one emotion to the next.

This subtlety in the music results in a rapid ping-pong game of action and reaction. It takes place between the singers and between the singers and the orchestra, then it moves into the audience and bounces back onto the stage. In the ensembles, the music brings everyone into focus, constantly shifting perspective. It's like a camera shooting from different angles, cutting from one shot to another, from close-ups to long shots. This forms the network of interactions that is typical of Mozart. In this regard it's also interesting to note that the emotional climax can be placed at very different points each time. In some arias it's even in the postlude (such as in Tamino's 'Bildnis' aria). Or the preceding recitative and the introduction to an aria can already reach such an emotional state that the singing seems to begin by itself (as in Susanna's 'Rose aria'). This variety has to be explored and carefully worked out.

Things can be easier in smaller opera houses such as those for which Mozart actually wrote his works. During my years at the Salzburg Festival, I discussed with several well-known architects what elements would constitute a 'Mozart theatre'. The main challenge, it transpired, would be to create a space that would facilitate this rapid ping-pong interaction between all the participants, including the audience. In big opera houses, everything becomes ponderous because the distances are too great. All reactions then lag behind the music, which is already far ahead. No one knew this better than Mozart himself, who composed his music accordingly. In the second act of *Figaro*, for example, Susanna hides on one side of the stage, behind the curtains at the window. After the Count and Countess have left the room, she has to use the introduction to her duettino with Cherubino to get as quickly as possible to the closet door on the other side of the stage in order to whisper frantically: 'Aprite, presto aprite' ('Open up, quick, open up'). When it's done at the proper speed, this introduction allows her to cover a distance of a maximum of twelve metres. On the stage of the world première in Vienna, the distance was eleven and a half metres.

In Mozart, the story is almost always already embedded in the musical structure. The presto clamour at the beginning of the overture to *Figaro*, for example, offers us an immediate impression of the 'folle journée', the 'crazy day' on which all the events come tumbling one on top of another. Additionally, Mozart shortens the opening phrase of the Overture by a single bar. So just when one would expect to hear the eighth bar of a regular musical period – whoops! – Mozart is already in the first bar of the following period, leaving us out of breath. The same technique of telescoping two musical periods is used later to a very different purpose in the 'letter duet' between the Countess and Susanna. Here, Mozart employs it to make audible the complete mutual understanding between these two women, beyond their social differences, once their interests have become identical. Their voices merge into each other so that one can barely tell where the one ends and the other begins. It couldn't be more feminine!

This is already part of a most essential element in Mozart: the position of his characters in the social fabric. Who is the master, who the servant? Who is rich and therefore powerful, and who is poor and therefore dependent? Who gives orders and who carries them out? Who conforms and who's rebellious? These societal issues are audible in the very structure of the music. The most famous example is in the first finale of *Don Giovanni*, where three orchestras on stage depict the social status of the different characters. The aristocracy has a minuet (in three-four time), the socially ambitious Zerlina dances a contredanse with Giovanni (in two-four time) while the peasants dance a crude 'Deutscher' (in three-eight time). It is therefore totally inadmissible *not* to put these three ensembles on the stage, regardless of what it costs, though it happens all the time in the brainless opera business.

Mozart's precise musical depiction of these social conditions has consequences in performance. Servants have to work and almost always have something to do, while the masters and mistresses have the time and the means to devote themselves to spiritual upliftment, or to engage in assorted pleasant pastimes. The servants usually have a more realistic approach to life, compared to the ideals of those born for higher things. This results in 'social gestures', i.e. attitudes and postures that are determined by the lives and work of the characters, and that set them off clearly, and dramatically effectively, from each other. And this in turn creates tension – for Mozart's servants are always rebellious. Where it's impossible for them to be directly disobedient, they do it indirectly. Blondchen and Pedrillo, Susanna and Figaro, Leporello, Masetto, Despina and of course Papageno all take every opportunity to criticize the social order and their masters, whether by speaking asides or by employing irony, sarcasm or exaggerated flattery. And their masters pay them back in kind – with arrogance, condescension and verbal abuse. 'Pazzo, mentecatto, vechia pretendente, razza di gente, birbo, mascalzon, ceffo da cani' ('Madman, lunatic, arrogant old spinster, riffraff, scoundrel, rascal, dog face') are just a few of the expressions used by the nobility to describe their personnel. Even Tamino expresses princely arrogance and painful immaturity in his scene with the Speaker in *The Magic Flute*. And the figures who are caught between those above and those below – such as Osmin, Basilio and Alfonso – engage in as much intrigue as they can in order to keep their heads above water.

These social contrasts were conventions in the older opera buffa, and Mozart made use of them just like everyone else who wrote for the theatre in his day. But he was able to fill these conventions with real, warm-blooded life in order to create the social cosmos of his works. In many of his letters we find firm opinions on social matters. They are notable for the same rebellious tone one finds in his operas, and they are garnished with angry outbursts, irony and biting sarcasm. This is hardly surprising for a man who was not only expelled from the degrading service of the Salzburg Archbishop with a kick in the behind but who also throughout his life placed great emphasis on respect and human dignity. As a Freemason, together with his Masonic brother Schikaneder, he brought to the stage in *The Magic Flute* the greatest social utopia of the eighteenth century (or, for that matter, of any century since): namely the everlasting union of power and justice. For Freemasonry had the same goals as the French Revolution – 'liberté, égalité, fraternité' – though it aimed to achieve them through evolution, not revolution, without the guillotine so to speak. Nor was Mozart simply a rebel who put slogans into music. His artistry united convention with revolution, thus making it far more comprehensive and timeless, right up to our own day.

A glance at *The Marriage of Figaro* may clarify this. At the end of the third act, a little revolution does indeed take place. The marriage has gone ahead without the Count being able to exercise his feudal rights and spend the wedding night with the newly married bride. The people celebrate Figaro and Susanna as the victors. They have achieved a small act of progress on the way towards a more just society and a greater respect for human rights. If Mozart were concerned only with this, the opera could have ended here. But he and his librettist Da Ponte take things much further. The real revolution occurs in the fourth act, outside societal boundaries, in the natural surroundings of the nocturnal park, under the revolving firmament and its laws of eternity. And the music revolves with it, swirling everyone about in its wake. When, however, everyone can be united in every possible erotic constellation – the noble and the lowly, the young and the old, the duped and the clear-sighted, whether disguised or not – then it becomes obvious how absurd, ridiculous and against nature are all barriers of social class, regardless of time or place.

Mozart's characters are intelligent. In the whole cosmos of his operas I have not found a single stupid person. It's this intelligence that produces the tensions in his work, in their constant alternations of attack and defence, advantage and disadvantage. It's relatively easy to get the better of stupid people, so it's not very interesting. But if the clever are in conflict with the intelligent, then things get exciting. In Mozart, everyone pursues his or her own interests and intentions in the most effective manner. For example, there is the gardener Antonio from *The Marriage of Figaro*, who is often – but wrongly – depicted as stupid and doltish. In fact, he's always right. He knows it, and insists on it. He didn't see a man on a horse jump out of the window: it wasn't so and he never said so. And he even offers a dose of critical sarcasm: if his master the Count insists that Cherubino is in Seville, then of course he is, as no one could argue against the Count; only in this case, Seville is in his own house. And in the *Entführung*, Osmin, his master's most faithful and vigilant servant, doesn't just claim he has 'a keen mind'. He also uses it cunningly and most dangerously.

Mozart's music takes them all seriously, which is why performers must never do down their character or engage in any clumsy, so-called 'comic' acting. Mozart's characters are smart, and they thrust and parry skilfully and elegantly. Their intelligent actions and reactions result in the texture of his music with its rapid shifts, its frequent oscillations between irony, sarcasm and deep emotion, its pitfalls and surprises. It's these that make the music so difficult for the performers. Because they, too, have to be intelligent in order to do justice to this music on stage. And ultimately, the audience also has to be intelligent – very intelligent indeed. At the very least, one has to assume they are.

Mozart's music also precisely depicts both the mental and the physical state of a character. Psychology and even physiology are transformed into music. The heart rate, bated breath, the tension in the muscles, the blood pressure, hormone production and adrenalin – all can be heard and comprehended in it. This is what makes Mozart's characters so full of life, and allows so many interpretations. Just as life cannot be lived in only one way, so a performer has many possibilities for interpreting a Mozart role. He can pick the one that's most promising in dramatic terms. For example, in the *Entführung*, the character of Konstanze gains considerably in depth if she plays out the inner conflict between her promise of fidelity to her fiancé Belmonte and her burgeoning love – against her own will – for the mature, fascinating Bassa Selim. The whole opera gains in depth from this. One doesn't have to perform the role in this way, but Mozart's music allows it, and in fact seems to support such an interpretation.

Like all great dramatists, Mozart exercises justice towards his creations. Performers have to pay careful consideration to this fairness, because it holds the whole cosmos of his works in balance. He constantly thinks and composes the opposite of what can be perceived. How convincingly justified is the evil schemer Basilio in *Figaro* through his aria about the 'skin of the ass' – he's just a little man who has to play dumb and shelter from the storms of life if he's going to survive. And what about the Count in the same opera? In his big aria – 'Allegro maestoso' – he plans to exert all his feudal power in order to crush Figaro and wrest Susanna from him. But already the music is buckling, and the woodwind howl with jealousy that Figaro should possess the woman 'che in me destò un affetto, che per me poi non ha' ('who has fired in me a passion that she then does not feel for me'). He is suffering deeply, so much so that we can feel pity for him and comprehend his wild bursts of anger. In this manner, all of Mozart's characters are depicted fairly on their own terms. Everything is true, as is also the opposite. This dialectical manner of proceeding – presenting thesis and antithesis at the same time – is found throughout Mozart's operatic œuvre. It gives his music an ambivalent character in many scenes, making it seem untrustworthy, even daemonic. At any time, this daemonic element can turn things upside down and prompt a catastrophe – or it can lurk in hiding, under a seemingly harmless surface. For example, at the beginning of *Così fan tutte* the two sisters show each other, crosswise, the pictures of their lovers and praise their virtues. It's all just a frivolous game in the clear sunshine of a lovely morning by the calm sea – and yet the devil is already showing his claws, as it were, even before the characters or the audience have noticed anything. Mozart's aim is to depict the drop height from this bright, carefree daytime to the hopeless, bitter, nocturnal end.

And, finally, Mozart also ventures to the very boundaries of the possible in one further respect with the question: just what can opera music – music for a purpose – actually achieve? How much contradictory content can it express at one and the same time without losing sight of its purpose – telling the story and depicting the events of the drama – and without confusing the listener? In other words: is it even possible to present Mozart's musical dialectic on stage in its totality? With music alone there would be no doubt about it, because different musical contents do not exclude each other. The simplest two-part musical composition is a perfect example of such a dialectic. But on stage? Is it at all possible to stage Mozart's play with simultaneous contradictions, his juggling of one truth with another? The opera singer's body is physically concrete. At any one time, it can produce only one expression, physically and vocally; he has only one source of breath. Unlike music, he cannot express one thing and its opposite at the same time. And even if he could, he would merely end up confusing the audience. But this is precisely what Mozart constantly demands: the simultaneous expression of one thing and its opposite. And that leads to the following questions: can music lie? Or can it tell the truth? Or both at the same time? Or one through the other? So which one is it? Which of the many truths should be shown, and how? And in what order, or in what combination? Trying to find this out is a task over which many have racked their brains. And this is why Mozart – the man asking these questions – is the ideal teacher of the crafty art of opera.

Useful rules

- ★ Take Mozart as your teacher. What you learn from him can be applied everywhere.
- ★ 'Mozart is a brain problem'. Train your 'switching speed' in Mozart.
- ★ Learn the 'micro-management' of music.
- ★ Play ping-pong! – action and reaction – with partners, orchestra and audience.
- ★ Determine how, in an ensemble, the ball is passed musically from one performer to the next.
- ★ Determine the emotional climax of an aria. Then shape it accordingly.
- ★ Define the social position of your character.
- ★ Servants and subordinates work.
- ★ Play every character as intelligently as possible.
- ★ Assume that the audience is intelligent, too.

★ Pay attention to the 'physiology' in Mozart's music, and adapt to it.

★ Choose the dramatically most effective version when playing a character.

★ Be fair; show all sides of a character and let the audience make its own judgement.

★ Include the opposite in your performance. Show that a scene could actually have a different outcome.

★ If the music doesn't take sides, let it keep its secrets.

L'italiana in Algeri, Gioachino Rossini, Schwetzingen Festival 1987, Zurich Opera 1987
Set designs for Acts I and II

Recitative

Recitatives are unloved by performers and audiences alike. People shorten them wherever feasible, and try to get over them as quickly as possible. Then they give a sigh of relief when they get to the next music number. That's a big mistake! Because the 'dry', 'secco' recitative, accompanied by just harpsichord and cello, is a wonderful invention halfway between spoken drama and opera. It gives singers much of the freedom that actors enjoy, allowing them to create their own performance 'score' while still giving them a harmonic and rhythmic frame within which they have to work. Recitative was at the very beginning of opera – the idea that spoken drama could be musicalized. For when it was first invented, opera was dominated by recitative. The drama was placed in the hands of music, which then – in the service of drama – developed its theatrical arsenal and gradually attained full power in opera as the principal means of expression.

In recitative, however, singers are free to adjust tempo, dynamics, tone colours, rests and punchlines as seems appropriate to their dramatic needs. And in recitative, musical time runs concurrently with narrative time. So the performer has to deliver his text in real time. Many singers who like to express emotions in expanded musical time are therefore no friends of recitative. But with the succession of recitative and aria, opera created the invaluable possibility of differentiating between news and commentary. The 'news' is unsuited to accompaniment by the orchestra, while the 'commentary', being a reflection on the news, demands a more emotional form of presentation in expanded musical time, with the full force of the orchestral accompaniment. Opera thus differentiates between what's worth knowing and what's worth feeling. Many masterpieces of the genre are animated by this very contrast, and if one disrupts the well-balanced equilibrium between the two, then one compromises their overall impact. Not to mention the fact that many of the traditional cuts in recitatives often eliminate core scenes that are essential to comprehending the whole work. This is common practice among dilettantes when masterpieces fail to match their own intentions.

Recitatives are difficult, and are made even more so because hardly anyone is taught how to deal with them. Their text simply has to be comprehensible. This demands a special technique: 'parlare intonato', literally 'speaking on the tone'. Instead there is usually too much singing, which makes recitatives incomprehensible in performance and devoid of the necessary subtlety. Preparing them properly demands a lot of time and patience. Recitative operas should therefore be assigned a longer rehearsal period – though this hardly ever happens.

Recitative is in fact the basis for all music theatre. It is both a training camp and a field of experimentation. Here a singer can develop all the abilities and techniques that he needs to become a music-actor. He doesn't have to force out any high notes, so instead he can concentrate on the dramatic reasons for what he has to deliver. Ask a singer to speak the text of a passage he has just sung. He'll almost always stumble and inwardly 'rewind' the music until he has found the text. For singers usually know the text only in connection with the notes, as if the text were merely a by-product of them. In principle this wouldn't matter, if they did not thereby deprive us of the reason behind both text and notes. Language and the music that goes along with it are actually a late end-product of a multitude of processes, from feelings both conscious and unconscious, of synapses firing in the brain, of nerves, the circulation, the glands and hormones. All these together create the thoughts that only at the very end are expressed as words and music. In evolutionary terms, too, language and music only evolved millions of years after all other natural means of expression had been developed. This is why, in life, the sequence of linguistic expression is invariably this: thinking – breathing – speaking. And so it must be on stage. It is within the relative freedom of recitative that one can best practise the ability to develop and express emotions and thoughts as the consequence of specific events and occurrences, an ability which then must be applied to the music as it has been composed, with its strict temporal and rhythmic conditions.

The sobriety of recitative forestalls any kind of emotional indulgence – which in any case is usually sham. My old cello teacher used to say: 'You can have feelings when you can play properly.' Recitatives compel us to be concrete and to ask: what exactly is happening? Who wants what from whom, and why? And where are the people and the places about whom I'm singing? If someone says: 'I'm going to the baker's, then to the butcher's', he has a precise notion of where the baker and the butcher are, and the path he has to take to get there. An opera singer needs to have a similarly precise spatial imagination. There's a good example of this in the Count's recitative at the beginning of the third act of *The Marriage of Figaro*, where he recapitulates the events of the second act – events which the audience has in part already seen and so can check on what he relates.

The Count is in the great hall of his castle. 'Che imbrazzo è mai questo!' (What an embarrassing confusion'), 'Un foglio anonimo' ('an anonymous note') – and here he imagines himself back in the courtyard where Basilio gave him Figaro's anonymous note, just as he was mounting his horse to go hunting. 'La cameriera in gabinetto chiusa, la padrona confusa' ('The chamber maid locked in the closet, the Countess confused'). Now he is recollecting the boudoir of the Countess and sees in his mind's eye the locked closet to the right, with the Countess in front of it, denying him entry. 'Un uom che salta dal balcone in giardino' (A man jumping from the balcony into the garden'). And here, he turns inwardly to the left, where the balcony window was, to which the indignant gardener Antonio had drawn his attention. 'Un altro appresso che dice esser quell desso' ('Another who claims it was him'). Now he once more lives through his surprise when Figaro – who was standing on the other side, with the Countess and Susanna – claimed he was the leaper from the balcony, and showed his sprained foot as proof of it. 'Non so cosa pensar' ('I don't know what I should think of all this'). And with this, the Count is back in his great hall, brooding over events.

News needs to be verified and credible – far more than the paramount emotions in a music number – so the recitative needs to know the biography of a character. What did he do before he appeared on stage? Where is he coming from, where is he going, what are his intentions? The more of this that is able to flow into the stage depiction of a character, the more credible and truthful he becomes. And what happens 'backstage', between his appearances? It is in such cases that a director can often give the composer a helping hand. For example, what exactly happened in far-off Burgos between Don Giovanni and Elvira, whom he had to marry in order to possess her? That's all the text says. So one must make use of everything that can be found out about her, from her own behaviour, from the reactions of others to her and, above all, from her music (see 'music detective'!) in order to explore her biography, which would make plausible her first vibrant appearance, bursting with energy and resolve. 'Cavare il cor' – she will tear out Giovanni's heart if he refuses to return to her. And then how she falls into an abyss of utter humiliation in the following scene, when she finds herself at roughly no. 987 in Leporello's catalogue of Giovanni's 1,003 Spanish lovers. It is in the recitative – where there is no thrilling music to carry the singer along – that knowing the biography, and incorporating that knowledge into performance, will offer a character depth, atmosphere and credibility.

There is an old theatrical saying in Germany that runs: 'listening pays half the rent'. That is especially true in recitatives. By just listening intently, reactions in both singer and addressee are prompted which make things livelier and more interesting for everybody involved, including the audience. This effect can be intensified by using the 'Huh?' technique. If the person being addressed seems not to understand and asks 'Huh?' (or even just thinks it), then he compels the speaker to express himself more clearly and vividly. If something surprising is communicated, one can also replace 'Huh?' with '*What*?!' This also allows for a 'double-take', the dual reaction when something is heard but not immediately understood. In this case, 'Huh?' and '*What*?' are combined together. 'Your wife is cheating on you.' 'Huh? – *WHAT*?!' This double-take isn't easy. The tiny pause between the two reactions is where the penny drops, and it has to be executed precisely. It can't be done mechanically, nor just aiming for a laugh from the audience. Only a dry, inner 'switch', like something snapping into place, can bring this off. Recitatives offer many opportunities for such reactions. And of course there are some wonderful composed-out double-takes in opera. One of the best is in *The Marriage of Figaro*, when the Count pulls back the cloth on the armchair where Cherubino is hiding – and realizes only from the reactions of the others present that something's up.

One can often link a recitative to an activity – with or without props. In *The Barber of Seville*, Figaro enters Doctor Bartolo's house in order to do Rosina's hair. He wants to tell her that 'Lindoro' (who is really Count Almaviva) is 'inamorato morto' ('dead in love') with her. And she wants to give Figaro the note she has already written to this 'Lindoro'. The two of them play an ironic cat-and-mouse game with each other, while Figaro brilliantly displays his virtuosity in the craft stated in the opera's title, for which he is so popular in Seville. His work proceeds either synchronously or counter-synchronously to the dialogue, and gives the whole scene an extra dimension that confirms the old theatrical wisdom: action leads the actor to the truth of his role.

And if an action is stopped because something new happens, this brings into play one of the most effective techniques for creating interest in the theatre: the interruption. The new is clearly more important than what had been going on before. If the interruption is caused by the entrance of a person, he or she becomes more interesting to the audience, prompting its curiosity. And of course, one can also humiliate the person entering by intentionally *not* interrupting what one is doing. This makes him appear unimportant, or assigns him to a lower social status. The type of interruption and the behaviour displayed straight thereafter allows one to read the social status and the personal relationships of the characters on stage. But an interruption can also create an atmosphere, such as when Hans Sachs wants to work on a balmy summer's night in Nuremberg, but is instead overwhelmed by the clarinets' tender scent of lilac ('Und doch, 's will halt nicht geh'n' – 'And yet it won't do') and begins his famous monologue – one of the highpoints of all operatic literature.

Recitatives often offer punchlines. They can all too easily be ruined by fumbling or fidgeting, but should instead be dropped nimbly like a ripe apple from a tree. A difficult art that's rarely mastered. Lies, irony and sarcasm are all employed, and often the singers have to think the opposite of what's being said (mostly rather nasty thoughts). In *The Marriage of Figaro*, for example, Susanna and Marcellina have a duet in which they shower each other with poisonous compliments. In a recitative, words or whole sentences can be expanded or coloured as one sees fit; one can imitate other people, characterize them as absurd or dangerous, or one can recite whole passages in a grandiloquent rhythm, only to plunge into banality – or into a general pause. But in the last case, one has to distinguish between a pause and a hole. A hole is dead; nothing happens in it. A pause, however, can encompass an entire world. It belongs to the music, it's one of its most tension-laden elements, and it's replete with energy. Pause and music belong together like matter and antimatter. But one has to master the pause in order to apply it effectively.

There is one more useful tip. If the text of a recitative is causing problems to the singer – either musically or emotionally – it can help to speak or sing it in his native dialect. Dialect is much closer to reality than is a literary language (or any foreign language, of course). Often, this will quickly fix things.

And then there's the art of addressing the audience. This has to be crafted like a cat-and-mouse game to be played with the thousand souls sitting in the auditorium. In *The Barber of Seville*, Figaro presents himself to the audience: 'Ha, ha, che bella vita!

Faticar poco, divertirsi assai, e in tasca sempre aver qualche doblone, gran frutto de la mia riputazione.' ('Ha, ha, what a lovely life! Not too strenuous, all the more pleasure, and in my pocket always a coin as the golden fruit of my reputation'). He says this to everyone, throwing his coin in the air and catching it skilfully. After this, he turns to the upper classes in their opera boxes: 'Ecco qua: senza Figaro non si accasa in Siviglia una ragazza' ('It's like this: without Figaro, no one in Seville marries off a girl'). Then, more intimately, he addresses a lady in the stalls: 'A me la vedovella ricorre pel marito' ('The young widow comes to me in search of a new husband'). Here he might even blow a discreet hand kiss in the direction of the lady. Then, turning back to everyone, he demonstrates his professional methods, presenting his comb and his guitar as his tools of work: 'Io, colla scusa del pettine di giorno, della chitarra col favor della note, a tutti onestamente, non fo per dir, m'adatto a far piacere' ('With the comb by day and the guitar under cover of night, I endeavour honestly – no need to mention it – to provide pleasure to everyone').

Figaro utters the aside about his honesty with a dash of stylish modesty, but then he erupts again: 'Oh che vita, che vita! Oh che mestiere!' ('Oh what a life, what a life! What a profession!'). Of course all this can be done differently – the only important thing is that Figaro conveys his bustling activity and his good mood in all their different facets to the audience, whom he always keeps in his grip like a lion tamer with his beasts in a circus.

The last element in the art of the recitative is its transition into the aria. Regrettably, one can often see how the singer relaxes self-contentedly at the final cadence of the recitative. He's done his duty, now it's the orchestra's turn with the introduction to the aria. And of course the audience does the same as him: they lean back and relax. All the tension that was built up in the recitative is now gone with the wind. Naturally, the transition to the aria can vary greatly according to the music and the dramatic situation. There might be a harsh contrast, or a gentle segue; it could be loud or soft; there could be a rest between the one and the other; or the aria might follow *attacca*, with no rest at all. But the singer must always stay in the breath of his character, maintain the tension and transfer it into the new music of the aria.

After all this, it should be obvious that recitatives aren't an inconvenient, obligatory exercise. No, they are the best training for the high art of dramatic representation in music. A singer who has mastered the recitative has usually mastered everything else too.

Useful rules

★ The (secco) recitative is important and must be worked out carefully.

★ Recitatives must be comprehensible. 'Parlare intonato!'

★ Find the reason behind the text and the music.

★ The sequence: thinking – breathing – speaking always applies.

★ Have an idea of where the people and things are that you're talking about.

★ Investigate and develop the biography of a character.

★ Define what happens 'behind the scenes' in between the appearances of a character.

★ 'Listening pays half the rent'.

★ Use the 'Huh?' and '*What*?!' techniques.

★ Practise double-takes.

★ Link the recitative to an activity. Use props.

★ 'Activity leads to the truth of a character'.

★ Use the technique of interruption.

★ Let punchlines drop casually like a ripe apple from a tree.

- ★ Don't ruin punchlines by fumbling and fidgeting.
- ★ Don't aim for laughs.
- ★ Make full use of the freedom a recitative allows – to expand, accelerate, add colour, illustrate, rhythmize, imitate or pause. Develop your imagination as a 'recitative composer'.
- ★ Learn the difference between pause and hole. Play with the pauses.
- ★ If you find a text difficult, say or sing it in your native dialect.
- ★ When addressing the audience, play 'cat-and-mouse' with them.
- ★ Put a high value on the transition from a recitative to an aria. Don't let there be a hole.

The Barber of Seville, Gioachino Rossini, Edinburgh Festival 1982, Cologne Opera 1982

Sketches of Figaro, Almaviva and Ambrogio

Being comic

What makes things comic? Characters on stage act with intentions. They hold opinions, they clash, they fight, they love, they laugh. Nobody is comic *a priori*. Whether or not we find something funny depends on the circumstances – perhaps there is a punchline, a contradictory situation, an unforeseen turn of events, a plunge from heady heights to the depths of the banal. Or just somebody slipping on a banana skin. Whatever it is, it's the audience who decides whether or not it's funny. Comic events might take place on stage, but their impact occurs in the auditorium. One and the same event can be comic or tragic – it just depends on the context and how it is perceived. Both can even apply at the same time – such as when Leporello reads out Don Giovanni's list of lovers to Donna Elvira. He finds it funny, while her whole world collapses in tragedy and the audience is torn between the one and the other. There are many such scenes that are all the more tragic, the funnier they are (and vice versa).

Fundamentally, there are two ways of achieving a comic effect. The one demands continuous fireworks with a punchline every twenty seconds. That is the way of boulevard comedy. One shouldn't dismiss it lightly, for it demands superior ability and a honed technique of dropping punchlines nonchalantly, or of juggling opposites such as big and small, slow and quick, pathetic and banal – as if pulling the rug out from under someone who's dressed to the nines.

The other, deeper and more comprehensive type of comic effect lies in situations, conditions, the character of people and their relationships to each other, and in the thrust of the whole story. This is how the great comedies achieve their impact. In fact, every great comedy is a thwarted tragedy. The essence of comedy lies in the 'lieto fine', the happy end, whether real or imagined. People feel: 'That was lucky, we've been saved by the skin of our teeth!'

The righteous burghers of Windsor, for example, are about to hang Falstaff from Herne's Oak when he recognizes Bardolfo at the last moment, thereby making everyone laugh. Ford says it out loud: 'By the gods, if I weren't laughing, you'd now be hanging up there!' Nothing is more wonderfully expressive of the comedic good luck of a happy end in the nick of time than Verdi's great closing fugue: 'Tutto nel mondo è burla' ('All the world's a joke').

In *The Marriage of Figaro,* Figaro has been condemned to pay back money he owes to the much older Marcellina straightaway, or else he has to marry her. The Count, as the supreme legal authority, confirms the ruling. Figaro is caught in a trap because he has no money. He fights like a rat in a cage and defends himself with the most absurd of arguments. He too was born into the nobility, he says, so he doesn't even fall under the Count's jurisdiction. His arguments become ever more outrageous. Everyone laughs at him and it all becomes too foolish for the Count, who waves him aside and turns around to leave. Figaro runs after him, and when the Count is already at the door he calls to him at the very last moment: 'E sopra tutto' – and above all, he's got a mark on his arm that proves his noble birth. Marcellina asks: 'In the shape of a spade?' Figaro: 'Yes, how do you know that?' At which Marcellina exclaims: 'Raffaello!' It's her own son, whom she had abandoned as a baby. It's a surprising comic twist. But if the Count had gone just one second earlier, and had Figaro been unable to mention the mark on his arm, what story would have emerged then? *King Oedipus* by Sophocles, the ancient tragedy at the very dawn of European theatre in which the son marries his mother and sires his own siblings. Just one second! This is how close comedy and tragedy are to each other.

The deadly sin of the comedian is therefore to sacrifice the truth of a character, a situation or a state of being, on the altar of comic effect. 'Can't we also be very serious while laughing?' asks Lessing in his comedy *Minna von Barnhelm*. One could also turn the sentence around: 'Can't we make people laugh while being very serious?' Comedy must be played intelligently for intelligent audiences, letting the laughs come of their own accord. One shouldn't try to instruct people when to laugh by employing the embarrassing, 'comic' ham acting that too often can be seen on the opera stage. Instead, one must convey to the audience that all great comedies teeter constantly on the brink of catastrophe. The happiness of comedy has a price – and that price is the dark, daemonic source from which tragedy springs.

Useful rules

- ★ Comedy is more difficult than tragedy.
- ★ Play comedies seriously.
- ★ Incorporate the possibility of tragedy when performing comedy.
- ★ Never sacrifice the truth of a character for a laugh.
- ★ Let the laughs look after themselves.
- ★ Never subvert your character.
- ★ Play with opposites, such as big/small, slow/quick, pathetic/banal.
- ★ Don't instruct the audience when to laugh.

La Cenerentola, Gioachino Rossini, Salzburg Festival 1988,
Royal Opera House London 1992

(top) Design for the proscenium *(bottom)* Set design for Act I

'Too many notes ...'

'Too many notes, dear Mozart, too many notes' is what Emperor Joseph II supposedly said after the first performance of the *Entführung aus dem Serail* in Vienna's old Burgtheater. Mozart's reply was: 'Just as many as necessary, Your Majesty.' This episode has served to condemn the poor Emperor as musically illiterate, but in fact the opposite was true. He was a decent cellist and every week in his Schönbrunn Palace he either listened to the latest chamber music or played it himself, all under the guidance of his court composers Gassmann, Salieri and Gluck.

Joseph actually could have gone down in history as one of the greatest theatre intendants, had his main job not been as Emperor of the Holy Roman Empire of the German Nation. While still the co-regent of his mother, the Empress Maria Theresia, he had founded the Burgtheater, which has remained to this day the premier German-language theatre. He systematically promoted the German *Singspiel,* the genre of comic opera whose most glorious fruit was Mozart's *Entführung*. The best contemporary composers wrote works for his Italian-language Court Opera under the direction of Antonio Salieri, and these works went on to enjoy huge success all over Europe. Besides Mozart, these composers included names such as Gluck, Haydn, Paisiello, Martin y Soler, Cimarosa and Salieri, who all wrote operas that are still performed today. And Lorenzo Da Ponte was just one of many librettists who were engaged to write for the opera – among the others were men as famous as Giambattista Casti, Goldoni and Beaumarchais. Not to forget Emanuel Schikaneder, who had originally come to Vienna with his theatrical troupe at the specific request of the Emperor himself, long before he wrote *The Magic Flute* with Mozart, and long before he built the Theater an der Wien and rose up to become the uncrowned king of theatre in the imperial capital. Many extant documents also prove that the Emperor busied himself with the details too. The copious instructions in his own hand that have survived include a note that the Stadler brothers – the first virtuosos on the clarinet and the newly invented basset horn – should be bound to Vienna by offering them good contracts, lest they be lured off to another court. To be sure, as Emperor, Joseph II had the power and the means to do all these things. But what a nose for talent he must have had, what an eye for vital developments that offered promise for the future!

Joseph's influence coincided with a unique constellation in the history of theatre. Never before or after were theatre and music, drama and opera as closely interwoven as in the opera buffa of the late eighteenth century. Today's clear distinction between actor and singer often did not apply at that time. Valentin Adamberger and Theresa Teyber, the first Belmonte and Blondchen in Mozart's *Entführung,* played Sergeant Werner and the chambermaid Franziska in Lessing's *Minna von Barnhelm* on the next night – two of the most demanding roles in the classical repertoire of German theatre. Nancy Storace, the first Susanna in *The Marriage of Figaro*, often switched from plays to operas later in her career when she was working in London. Francesco Benucci, the first Figaro (and later Leporello in *Don Giovanni* and Guglielmo in *Così fan tutte*), was admired as much for his singing as for his acting. And Schikaneder himself, the librettist of *The Magic Flute* and the first-ever Papageno, was a veritable all-round man-of-the-theatre who was also a first-rate Shakespearean actor, famous especially for his Hamlet. And the list could go on.

The existence of this type of singer-actor was what made the opera buffa masterpieces possible in the first place – many of which were composed in Vienna under Joseph. The musical–dramatic style of these works, with their constant, rapid shifts of expression, requires just such singer-actors in possession of both a virtuoso vocal technique and a subtle mastery of the dramatic arts. Ideally, the characters in these operas should be depicted as wholly credible human beings in all their individual and social relationships, just as they would be depicted in a play by Goldoni or Lessing, with only one difference: the drama has here been musicalized.

So what did the Emperor mean by 'too many notes, dear Mozart?' He was obviously trying to find a polite way of saying 'Dear Mozart, you're cheating a bit. You've put many elements of the drama into the orchestra, elements such as character, status, mood, nuances of expression and even the subconscious, all of which ought to be the business of the interpreter on the stage.' Franz Schubert once remarked that his revered teacher Salieri had little respect for people who overloaded the orchestral accompaniment in opera. He was probably referring to Mozart, and His Majesty's opinion had surely been influenced by his Court Capellmeister. According to Salieri, music's purpose in opera was 'to support the drama' – in other words, to offer a broad outline to the performers, but otherwise leave them a free hand to develop their roles. That is precisely how all the other composers of the time worked, each after his own fashion. But Mozart broke this convention. He did things differently, by giving the orchestra an independent role alongside that of the performer on stage. This meant that he took away some of the performer's freedom, and tied him closer to the musical score. The Emperor seems to have noticed this straightaway in Mozart's first opera for Vienna, which proves how keen his musical instincts were. From today's perspective it almost makes him seem equipped with prophetic gifts.

Opera now underwent an evolution in which the orchestra became ever more emancipated and important. In Mozart, there was still a perfect equilibrium between singers and orchestra. But then the balance shifted more and more to the orchestra. The number of instruments in it rose accordingly, which in turn meant that bigger, more dramatic voices became necessary. At the same time, the singers lost more and more control over their own performance. This is already obvious in the Wolfsschlucht scene in Weber's *Freischütz*, whose Romantic frissons and terrors are brought forth by the orchestra alone. Then Richard Wagner came along, not only assigning the orchestra the task of depicting present events as they happen on stage but linking them to the past and the future through his system of leitmotifs. He thereby created relationships and significance, loading the orchestra with psychology, dreams and the unconscious. All this left little autonomy for the performer on stage, who became a slave of the orchestra and has to conform to what it commands. In *Tristan and Isolde*, Brangäne has to give the lovers their supposed death potion in the exact bar, on the exact quarter note, when the orchestra plays the 'death motif' – which is at the same time an inversion of the opera's opening love motif. And even a dramatically clueless bass can become an overwhelming King Marke because the tragedy and its harrowing impact take place in the orchestra with its mysterious, dark colours and characteristic sound of the bass clarinet.

And then onto Richard Strauss. In *Elektra* or *Die Frau ohne Schatten*, the orchestra is so overladen with 'psychological polyphony', with 'counterpoint of the nerves' as Strauss himself called it, that only experts can understand all that's happening in it. To be sure, the audience is overwhelmed by the expansive melodies, the glittering orchestration, the rhythmic power and emotional impact of it all. But they hardly comprehend anything of the 'grammar', the actual content of the orchestral language. Even the singers, who are supposed to be acting out what's in the music, rarely have a clue as to what's really going on.

This is what once happened in a rehearsal for *Elektra*, in the central scene between the title character and her mother Clytemnestra. The latter was being sung by one of the great singer–actresses – a wonderful stage-tigress. Clytemnestra, who murdered her husband Agamemnon with an axe in his bath, now suffers from nightmares. 'Allein es lässt sich vertreiben' ('But they can be driven out'), she sings. I suggest: 'Look at Elektra here – your words seem harmless, but they're a threat. It can clearly be heard in the orchestra, the threefold falling motive of the axe. What Clytemnestra really means is: if you don't stop accusing me, the same axe can deal with you just like with your father.' After a moment of surprise, the great singer replied: 'Why should I care about that music?'

This might seem just a joke. But the fact remains that singers are often overtaxed by what is happening in the orchestra. In subsequent developments up to the present day, many important operatic works have failed to develop any comprehensible orchestral syntax for the events that they are depicting on stage. This is precisely the reason for the difficulty audiences have with contemporary opera.

Joseph II could never have dreamed of all this. And yet he addressed a fundamental aspect of all operatic endeavour, namely: what has to be said on stage, and what in the music? What are the singers communicating, and what the orchestra? When are they complementing each other, when are they in opposition? Who is yielding to whom – sometimes even to the point of total silence? This relationship is different from one composer to the next, from one opera to the next, even from one scene to the next. It's a relationship that must be explored afresh every time.

Richard Strauss once gave a one-sided but succinct answer to this (in his own favour) at a rehearsal for a festive performance of *Salome* in Zurich. He himself was conducting, and the director was no less a man than Walter Felsenstein – the same who later wrote operatic history at his Komische Oper in Berlin. They reached the point where Jochanaan pushes Salome away and retreats into his cistern. In the ensuing interlude, Salome hurtled across the stage in anger, then threw herself onto the grating of the cistern, her every gesture matching the accents of the music, all meticulously staged by Felsenstein. Here Strauss interrupted and asked: 'Mr Felsenstein, what's all this for?' Felsenstein came swiftly to the orchestra balustrade and embarked on a detailed explanation. 'You see, Herr Dr Strauss: she's hurt – she's still half a child, but is already aware of her femininity, and her frustration works its way through her in long runs across the stage until everything comes together on the cistern in her one decisive idea: "I want the head of Jocha–"' – at which Strauss interrupted him, unmoved. 'But what do you want, Herr Felsenstein?', waving a hand towards the orchestra, 'I do all that.'

Useful rules

- ★ Determine what the music says, and what the stage action says.
- ★ When must you show something, and when can you let the music show it?
- ★ When is the performer a slave of the orchestra? And when is the music a servant of the action?
- ★ What can be left out because the audience knows it anyway?

La gazza ladra, Gioachino Rossini, Cologne Opera 1984, Théâtre des Champs-Élysées Paris 1988

Set designs for Acts I and II

Dramaturgy

'And what do you hope to achieve with this?' I still remember his Augsburg dialect whispering in my right ear. It was the voice of Caspar Neher, that great man of the theatre: set designer, librettist, friend and colleague of Bertolt Brecht who had immortalized him in several poems. Neher had sat himself behind me at the director's desk, had watched me at work for a while, and then this: 'And what do you hope to achieve?' It felt like having a bucket of cold water poured over me and made me start all over again. For some reason or other, Neher had directed his *furor pedagogicus* at me. And what a pedagogue he was! His lessons were strict, and often spiced with irony and sarcasm.

'We need one more chair', I said in the dusty furniture storage room. 'What kind of chair?' he asked promptly. 'Empire style would be best', I suggested. 'Really. What do you mean by "Empire"?' I quickly sketched a chair. 'Here, Empire, you see ... Napoleon.' 'Aha. So you mean Louis XVI.' And so it went on the whole day.

Once, we were walking through the garden of the Belvedere in Vienna when he stopped at the steps that lead up to Prince Eugen's magnificent palace. He took out a small ruler that he always kept with him. 'Measure it!' – 'What?' – 'The steps!' – '47 × 11.5 centimetres.' 'If you ever want elegant steps', he said, 'use these', at which he stuck his ruler back in his pocket. On another occasion, he grumbled: 'I'll take any colour as long as it's grey.' And he went on to explain that nature generally prefers muted colours. It uses strong, luminous colours only as a signal meaning 'Mate with me!' or 'I'm poisonous, don't eat me!' Accordingly, he believed that theatre should use colours in the same way. Neher was the most merciless, incorruptible dramaturge I ever met.

Dramaturgy – it's a grand word that often lacks a proper meaning. How much nebulous gibberish comes along with it! And yet dramaturgy is really something quite simple: what has to be said, and how it must be said to be understood. What do the author and his work, and the performer with his interpretation, want to tell the audience? Between these three participants in every performance – the author, the performer and the audience – mediation is needed. Dramaturgy, as the mother of all dramatic arts, provides clarity, orientation and comprehensibility.

Opera, however, doesn't much like the discipline this mother imposes. It doesn't want to be understood. After all, it's got music, which addresses the emotions directly, without any need of intellectual understanding. Opera's musical and pictorial splendour allows it to soar above all reasoning, like Phaeton in his sun chariot. And yet without the reins of dramaturgy, this ascent into the heavens all too often ends crashing to earth. Being unconscious of itself, opera needs the aid of dramaturgy in order to comprehend itself. It's not a lack of talent that causes most operatic catastrophes, but a lack of dramaturgical thinking. And conversely, good dramaturgy is regrettably rarely noticed in opera. Nevertheless, without self-reflection and some common sense – to sum it up: without a minimum of philosophy – even opera can't exist.

The dramaturge (who in the English-speaking world also variously goes under the title of 'director of drama and text' or 'editorial coordinator') has to combine the materiality, physicality and unambiguousness of the stage with the immateriality, intangibility and ambiguity of the music. It's not an easy task. Primarily, this is the job of the stage director, most often in collaboration with the set designer. And if they are joined by a critical dramaturge, then they form an ideal team. Many dramaturges offer valuable, welcome knowledge about the history, reception history and biographical background of a work, and can put it all into clever articles for the programme book. But there are very few who are able to contribute directly to the practical work on stage during the production process. Apart from Caspar Neher, I knew only Friedrich Dürrenmatt, Angelus Seipt (who died far too young) and one or two others who could do this.

Dramaturgical thinking isn't only intellectual reflection such as one usually associates with 'thinking', but an associative process involving all five senses: feeling, listening, observing, tasting and smelling – with 'thinking' added as a sixth sense. A lot takes place in the twilight of the subconscious. The right conceptual solution can sometimes be prompted suddenly by the scent of a good wine or the sight of a brightly glittering object, neither of which has anything to do with the thing at hand itself. Or the catalyst might be a vigorous quarrel. Sometimes it all goes very quickly, but at other times one can agonize for half a year without achieving any usable result in this 'alchemist's kitchen'.

The natural prerequisite for the dramaturge is a precise knowledge of the work and the score. All the techniques of the 'music detective' have to be applied in order to find out what is meant, in the details as well as over the entire work. All the information that can contribute to the understanding of the work has to be gathered: the history of its conception, the circumstances, intellectual trends and fashions of the time, biographical data about the authors and, last but not least, a precise analysis of the harmonic and formal aspects of the music. All this groundwork is important in helping to understand a work. But it's relatively unimportant when it comes to the practical work of transforming it into flesh and blood on stage. Here, only imagination controlled by dramaturgy can help.

Because, with certain exceptions, the work is an information system complete in itself. It can offer only the information that is already inherent in it. It doesn't change. What does change are the circumstances in which the work is performed – the generations that come afterwards with their own performers and audiences, who all have their own life experiences from the times they live in. This is what changes the perspective of a work created long ago. It is all the more the case because the great works of art encompass such an abundance of information, different points of view, characteristics and contradictions that later generations will find one or another of them significant and bring it to the fore. Since every individual also looks at such a work differently, according to his or her own ideas and experiences, many different interpretations emerge quite of their own accord. When the zeitgeist, topical fashions and self-centred subjectivism are also added to the mix, it can seem as if these works are mutable at will and are open to anything and everything. These zeitgeist fashions can then very quickly transmute into hard-line dogma, proclaiming alternative perspectives as old-fashioned and inadmissible.

Very soon, however, such subjectivism usually falls victim to ridicule. For the great works seem to possess a far higher degree of objectivity than is generally supposed. The importance of any interpretation, necessary and inevitable as it may be, is vastly exaggerated. Great stories and great music are usually indestructible and triumph easily over the zeitgeist. Once more: the works themselves don't change. Changes lie in the eye and ear of the beholder. It's not the work that must adapt to the subjective view of its interpreter, but its interpretation that must adhere to the objective structure of the work – in opera mainly that of the music. If that doesn't suit one, then one must write a different work!

Here, finally, comes the 'R' word that's a thorn in the flesh to many: *Regietheater* – 'director's theatre'.

This is a type of theatre that has conquered the stages of the world in recent decades. *Regietheater* in and of itself isn't any better or worse than any other kind of theatre. It's theatre in which the director isn't there to serve the work, but in which the work becomes the raw material to which the director may add his own ideas, notions, fantasies and associations, independent of the actual form and structure of the work. This means that the work may be arranged, altered, transformed, mixed with other materials, and shortened or lengthened. Out of this – as in any kind of theatre – very bad or very wonderful theatrical experiences can result. To give one example: the great director Peter Brook wanted to tell the story of *Carmen*, but differently from Bizet. All the same, he found that a lot of Bizet's music could be useful to him. So he took the numbers that suited him, had them rearranged, mixed them together with his own material and put it all in his new production. The result was a fascinating evening of theatre.

If any of those in attendance were afterwards able to see a good performance of Bizet's original *Carmen*, they were doubly blessed. One thing, however, should be pointed out: Peter Brook was honest in his credits, calling his production 'La tragédie de Carmen, par Peter Brook, d'après Georges Bizet' ('The tragedy of Carmen, by Peter Brook, after Georges Bizet'). And indeed, *Regietheater* shouldn't water down a good wine, but put an honest label on the bottle. Then the world can decide whether the original is better, or the interpretation offered by the *Regietheater*. Or, as in the case of Brook/Bizet, that both are really good.

It's also very debatable whether the biography of the composer can be added to an opera, as it is often done. Wagner's relationship with Mathilde Wesendonck might have been his reason for composing *Tristan and Isolde*, but Isolde doesn't know that. And her duped husband isn't called Otto, but Marke. *Tristan* isn't a *roman à clef* in which it would help to peek through the keyhole. I also recall a performance of Othmar Schoeck's *Penthesilea* in which a gilded concert grand piano was hung over the Amazons' battlefield. The review of the next day enlightened me: the composer had been in a passionate affair with a lady pianist that had ended in torment – whereupon he had composed *Penthesilea*, the tragic story of the Amazon queen whose raging passion leads her to kill her beloved Achilles, tearing him apart with her teeth together with her pack of dogs. Hence the gilded grand piano!

Just as dubious is the common trend of incorporating the reception history of a work into a production. There is no doubt that Wagner strongly participated in the anti-Semitism that was widespread among the bourgeoisie of his time, just as his tendentious essay *Das Judenthum in der Musik* (*Jewishness in music*) laid the foundations for the dreadful misuse of his works by the Nazis. No question, either, that he vented his anger against the prominent critic Eduard Hanslick by using a variant of the man's name for the Nuremberg *Stadtschreiber* (town clerk) in the first version of his libretto for *Die Meistersinger*. But Wagner was too great an artist not to delete this biographical detail from the final version, where his pedantic clerk has become 'Beckmesser'.

Die Meistersinger as it stands has nothing to do with anti-Semitism, let alone Nazism. It even puts a higher value on the survival of art than on the survival of the nation. The metamorphosis of life into art is in fact the most important element of any creative process, but if art is to be great and achieve universal validity, it may not know anything about the individual circumstances of its author and must be detached from its subjective origins. Dredging up these details and mixing them into the performance of the work might (possibly) result in interesting theatre for insiders. But its appeal will be manifest more in the programme book than on the stage itself. It will be couched in a language largely for initiates and incomprehensible to the general public, because the audience knows nothing about the lady pianist nor about Wagner's vendetta against Hanslick.

Nor should the audience *need* to know all this, because none of it is actually in the libretto or the score. And it's these two things that the dramaturge has to take as the basis of his interpretation. As a child of his time he will automatically add his own layer of subjectivity to the objectivity of the work. He will try to find out what the work means by reading it from a contemporary perspective and interpreting it on its own inherent terms, in order to bring the objective information offered by text and score into harmony with his own subjective ideas and associations. Then he will present his result on the stage, where the work will be reflected in the perspective of every individual in the audience. Given such a dizzying number of perspectives it is natural that a broad spectrum of interpretations will be possible. The decisive criterion is whether the result makes sense – and whether that sense is properly communicated and comprehensible. Who wants what from whom, and why, is the basis of understanding. Without it, the audience can't 'participate' in the events on stage. For an audience has two fundamental possibilities: identification or alienation. With the former it shares in the fate of Romeo, willing him to climb up onto Juliet's balcony, safe and undiscovered; with the latter, it disapproves of his love-struck foolhardiness because it's dangerous and can only end in death. The audience can oscillate very rapidly between these two attitudes – but only if it comprehends the reason and the purpose of the whole endeavour.

In this context I should mention the question I'm often asked when I plan a production: 'Will it be traditional or modern?' In return, I then ask what is meant by 'modern'. But I rarely get a proper answer. So I offer the questioner a crutch. Do we agree that the people in the audience are alive today – in other words, that they are contemporary, 'modern' people? Of course they are – so everything that touches them, moves them, excites them or angers them, making them laugh or cry, obviously has to be modern. And anything that doesn't have this impact on them, but instead bores them, leaves them uninterested or indifferent, must be un-modern. In short: 'modern' is something that is decided more in the auditorium than on stage. The content and the purpose of a work can be presented in all kinds of ways, but it all has to make sense to the contemporary, 'modern' people in the audience.

Despite the immense variety of possible interpretations, there are still limitations, such as when outside ideas are grafted onto a work that are simply not in tune with the actual content of it. When the work has the misfortune not to conform to the opinions of its interpreter, the result is usually devoid of sense. In *The Marriage of Figaro*, for example, the basic problem lies in the fact that one person possesses all the power and all rights, while the others have none. So how can they assert themselves? How can they defend themselves when their fundamental human rights are threatened by the whims of a single man? The whole plot is founded on this constellation. It depends on a society that is based on this disparity. To situate the action in a modern, democratic state would deprive the story of any sense, because people could just call the police.

Of course an opera can be removed from the original time and place of its plot, but then a well-developed understanding and awareness of the music is needed, because the music can express the specific atmosphere and mood of a scene better than any words. Unmusical bumbling can ruin everything. One also has to be careful when transposing the action to a place of which opera people generally have no experience whatsoever: atomic power stations, concentration camps or suchlike. The result can be ridiculous – or, even worse, it can offend those people who possess the requisite knowledge or have even suffered there themselves.

The same applies to topics that are in fashion at any one time and so are smuggled into a defenceless work. Critiques of capitalism are a popular theme today. But if one probes these doughty anti-capitalists, one gets a few surprises. Not that one should expect them to have read Marx's *Das Kapital,* but they should at least have some basic knowledge of economics. To have read some essay or other by Adam Smith or John Maynard Keynes, or to have some clue about the general vocabulary of the world of finance. Or that maybe they themselves have won or lost money through investments. But one finds nothing of the sort. Apart from the fact that 'capitalism' isn't necessarily suited to musical treatment in the first place, these anti-capitalist critics generally know nothing, can prove nothing, and have experienced nothing of it. All they can offer is a well-meaning, blabbering spectacle dripping with righteous moral indignation. But 'meaning well' is contrary to art. If art – let alone opera – can lay claim to any morality, then it can be measured only by the precision with which it depicts things. To take the audience for fools isn't moral. And foolishness should be avoided, because – as Bert Brecht put it – 'foolishness makes fools of those that encounter it'.

What's more, it makes people unmusical. A young director once came to me when I was an intendant. He wanted to stage a production of *Lohengrin,* but found the title character far from positive. He arrives on stage in all his shining splendour, equipped with the power of the Grail, he gives a thrashing to the dutiful state prosecutor who is just trying to clear up a murder case, and immediately everyone is screaming 'Heil ... our Führer!'. That had been done enough before. So my young director was convinced it was now his moral duty to present Lohengrin as a dull, threatening thug. I replied that I would find this reading plausible – but then the dull thug shouldn't appear to the sound of silvery trumpets in A major like he does in Wagner. It would be far better to do it in f-sharp minor, with saxophones. Because in opera, if one turns a stage event on its head, then one has to do this with the music too, given that the music has to express what happens on stage. Seeing the shocked look on his face, I took the argument one step further. Yes, he should go ahead and change the score. As his intendant, I'd stand alongside him during the ensuing public uproar, because after all, he wouldn't actually be harming Wagner's score, which would still remain the same on the printed page. He could create a living theatrical experience under the honest title of *Lohengrin* by X, using music by Wagner, arranged by Y for performance in Z. Whether or not my young colleague decided he couldn't do it or wouldn't do it, the production never came about.

If, as in this case, the actual score is contrary to the ideas of the director, then he should either put aside his ideas or put aside the music and try his hand at another art form. Walter Felsenstein, the great reformer of opera, summed it up simply: 'Music that does not grow out of the action on stage has nothing to do with theatre. And action that does not identify precisely and artistically with the music should rather dispense with the music altogether.'

But opera is happy with itself and doesn't really want to know about such basic principles. Instead it prefers to retreat into the sphere of music as its fundamental element. In doing so it denies its very nature, forgetting the purpose of its music and relying instead on its sheer beauty of sound. And audiences willingly let themselves be seduced by it, not bothering further about the absurdity and often the sheer unmusicality of what they see on stage, but instead just shutting their eyes and abandoning themselves to the magic of the music. Because in its essence and impact, music is indeed a magical art that can put human beings into a state of trance, opening them up to unknown psychic spaces. But at the same time it plays with the magic of numbers of the most refined construction and speculative impact. Thus music can suspend the dualism of identification and alienation. The knowledge of its construction can move us deeply, even to a point of ecstasy. Clarity and magic mutually enhance each other and become a unity. In this regard, Wagner speaks of 'Gefühlsverständnis' ('emotional understanding') as the real receptive organ for opera. And he felt nothing but contempt for 'Wirkungen ohne Ursachen' ('effects without causes'). For him, 'Every bar of music in a drama is justified only by expressing something relevant to either the action on stage or the character doing the action.'

This demand on Wagner's part opens up a vast field for dramaturgy. How does one find out what is 'relevant'? What belongs and what doesn't? Where is the interface between the four possibilities of 'good', 'bad', 'right' and 'wrong'? For it can happen that something is good but wrong, or right but bad. And there is one more fourfold tier on top of this: 'interesting' – 'boring' – 'truth' – 'lies'. It is all an equation with many unknown factors. Every possibility that is realized means excluding many others. Often, several important motifs are set in the score at the same time – such as is often the case in Richard Strauss or Alban Berg. But only one of them can be represented in the action.

Oh, one just wants to cry: *damn the physical unambiguousness of the stage!* What can we see and hear? And what can we only hear, but can't see? What does the music know, what's it keeping secret, what associations is it offering? Often the music knows more about the characters than they do themselves. Siegmund and Sieglinde barely know each other by the time the orchestra is telling us prophetically about their son and his sword. When is the music expressing emotions, when is it commenting on the action, and when is it doing both? Once again: *damn the ambiguousness of the music!*

How should we calculate the drop height of a tragic fall from grace? How should we work out a twist that takes us from the serious to the comic? How does the music depict the hero? It often does it bombastically, although true heroes are usually weak people who have to overcome their fears in order to achieve something seemingly impossible – like Leonore in *Fidelio*. Then there are all the practical issues of how to realize this on stage. The text of the libretto is the basis of both action and music, a kind of skeleton of the drama. But the audience rarely understands it, because too few singers articulate properly. What can be done to better understand the text in order to comprehend the music? What's more, the custom today is to perform operas in their original language. But if the audience can't understand the language in which the work is sung, it can't judge the sense and plausibility of what's happening on stage. This fact alone has opened wide the doors of opera for the charlatans. So we have to have surtitles. Or should it all be sung in translation, such as was the norm forty years ago before the globalization of opera? Both these possibilities have advantages and disadvantages, and also have an impact on the style and aesthetic of a production. Indeed – style and aesthetics! People speak more about these two aspects than they do about the content, precision and truth of the stage representation. And yet style and aesthetics are the end result of all these issues.

And finally: where can we trust the composer blindly, and where do we have to give him and his work a helping hand? For even Mozart makes mistakes! Even he had to compose twelve operas before he managed to write his first masterpiece, *Idomeneo* (and not even this is faultless). Not to mention *Don Giovanni*, with a libretto that Da Ponte had half-plagiarized from Bertati. The poor man himself describes proudly in his memoirs how he had to write three libretti at the same time. The first was for the almighty opera director Salieri, the second for Martin y Soler, the composer of successful operas. That just left him time in the evening to write for Mozart, which he could only do with the aid of a 'charming servant girl', as he himself put it.

Dramaturgical thinking is something that develops only slowly. Young geniuses are rarely to be found here. It takes time to set yourself free from the urge to be interesting and eye-catching. It takes time to nurture the necessary critical attitude towards your own 'brilliant' ideas, and instead to learn how to develop them out of what's actually in the libretto and the score, realizing that superficial ideas are in fact 'effects without causes', and putting your own person behind the task of interpreting a work, not in front of it. It takes time to cultivate the sober, utilitarian thinking that characterizes a good dramaturge – the ability to ask Neher's question 'And what do you hope to achieve with that?' Only then will you be in a position to answer the many difficult, often contradictory questions that the work poses. They are enough to make the dramaturge dizzy. He might then remember what an old, much-loved actor in the Burgtheater used to say to his prompter when he couldn't remember his text: 'No details, dear – just the work!'

The work! Dramaturgy is the mother of the work, and she has to look after her child, defending it against all unreasonable demands of everyday business, against false traditions (what Gustav Mahler called 'Schlamperei', 'sloppiness'), against amateurism, against the vanity of its performers, against the commercial interests of their agents and often against the false expectations of the audience too. Like Hans Sachs, a dramaturge has to be 'Schuhmacher und Poet dazu' ('a shoemaker and a poet too'). He has to possess both analytical skills and a profligate imagination if he is to protect opera from the business of opera. His task is to let the work and its performers flourish, and then to step back himself and become invisible.

Useful rules

★ The basic question is: what is to be said, and how, so it might be understood?

- ★ The basic prerequisite is: a precise knowledge of the libretto and the score.
- ★ Tools: use everything that helps you to understand the work.
- ★ Read the work from a contemporary perspective, and interpret it on its own inherent terms.
- ★ Play for the audience, not for insiders, critics or the media.
- ★ The basis of understanding is: who wants what from whom, and why?
- ★ If you adapt a work, label it honestly.
- ★ 'Modern' is decided in the auditorium.
- ★ Don't make claims about things you don't understand. If you *do* want to understand them, go and learn about them.
- ★ A major change to the story implies a change to the music. Action and music must depend on each other.
- ★ Understanding music's structure increases music's emotional power.
- ★ Definitions: good – bad, right – wrong; interesting – boring, truth – lies.
- ★ Create the 'drop height' and emphasize contrasts.
- ★ Heroes are people who can't really do what they end up doing. They are weak and have to overcome their fears.
- ★ Truth and clarity come first. Style and aesthetics are a result of them.
- ★ Find out where the composer and his work can be helped.
- ★ Practise dramaturgical thinking. It takes time and patience.
- ★ The work is the star. Everyone else is a servant.

La gazza ladra, Gioachino Rossini,
Cologne Opera 1984, Théâtre des Champs-Élysées Paris 1988

Sketch of peasant women

Breaking the rules

'Thou shalt not make unto thee any graven image, or any likeness of any thing that is in heaven above, or that is in the earth beneath, or that is in the water under the earth.' It was with a violation of this Commandment that theatre began. Because theatre people, whether they want to or not, must make a precise image of all that is in heaven and earth, if necessary even of the Almighty Himself and also of his Adversary. There's no other way about it. So it's off to hell with us all! Unless a compassionate archangel (I like to think it would be my namesake, Michael) points out that breaking this Commandment has actually produced unfathomable 'high works' to the glory of the Almighty and His creation (thus do They speak in heaven, according to Goethe). God cannot create Man after His own image and then proceed to extinguish the divine creative spark by imposing impossible commandments on him. So before the poor people of the theatre are sent to hell – they have a tough enough time on Earth anyway! – the Almighty should visit the opera and convince Himself of the glory of its works. The answer to this putative archangelic argument is still open, right down to the present day.

Since breaking the above Commandment in times immemorial, theatre has broken every other rule too. The contrast of rule (thesis) and breaking the rule (antithesis) always produces something new (synthesis) that unites elements of both. This dialectic always was, and remains, the motor of artistic development. This applies both to the individual artist and to whole genres.

So why the need for rules at all, if they're to be broken and replaced with new ones anyway? Well, just imagine a game (which is what opera is too), but without rules. Think of football. If one could kick the ball anywhere, anyhow, there would be no point to it, no consequences, and it would very soon be boring and stupid. It's only the rules – applied and understood by players and spectators alike – that make the game exciting. How team A competes against team B, within the framework of the rules, but with surprising new combinations and with infringements being punished. This is just the same as the fundamental dramatic constellation of theatre. One person wants something; another wants the opposite; and there's a third one who judges them.

So rules are founded on an agreement in which everyone comes together ('convenire') and to which everyone adheres: in other words, rules are founded on *conventions*. Every game and every genre has its own conventions that encapsulate the experience and wisdom of generations. They are guidelines for functioning correctly. They are very necessary, and not at all negative. Nietzsche understood this: 'Every mature art has a wealth of conventions as its basis ... conventions are the condition for great art, not a hindrance to it' (*The will to power*).

Conventions are bad only when they are applied uncritically, or dogmatically decreed to be non-negotiable. In both instances, this hinders playing freely with them. For conventions actually allow a lot of free space, with an inestimable number of possible moves and combinations, just like in a game of chess. This is what gives them their appeal. Conventions have never hindered a genius from playing with them. The long-held architectural convention of a building with a large central block and two side wings never prevented Michelangelo, Bernini or Schinkel from making exciting contributions to the development of architecture.

The traditional form of the aria, along with the sequence of 'recitative–aria' and the culminating finale, were long recognized in opera as a mature compositional convention. But that never stopped a great composer from writing a masterpiece. By exploring ever new combinations over the course of time, these conventions too evolved and developed, again offering new possibilities as they did so. The genre develops through this constant interplay of conventions and their manipulation.

The opposite of such an evolution is a revolt: a radical break with the rules. If it is genuine, it happens out of a need. An artist who looks and feels deeper, with more intensity, must inevitably experiment and break with tradition in order to find the right expression for his new vision. 'Nun sang er wie er musst'; und wie er musst' so konnt' er's' ('He sang as he had to, and as he had to, so he could'), sings Hans Sachs in Wagner's *Meistersinger*. What's astonishing about this is that the greatest, most radical rule-breakers were also the ones who knew and mastered the rules best. Like Wagner, who wrote a piano arrangement of Beethoven's Ninth Symphony in order to assimilate it totally, or – closer to our own time – Hans Werner Henze, who knew his way around old Italian madrigals like almost no one else. They all knew where they came from, and to whom they owed their abilities. And when they broke the rules they created new, expanded ones in the process – sometimes even stricter than the old ones (Schoenberg, for example). This leads us to conclude that it might also be a mistake in opera to ignore all conventions and traditions. After all, the word 'tradition' actually signifies something highly progressive and reasonable. Its root, 'transire', means to proceed, to go beyond, to a distant shore – but remaining aware of where one comes from and why one is taking the next step. Innovation can certainly be combined with tradition, but it need not arrive in turmoil. The new, integrated with the old, is usually far more effective and revolutionary than any strident shrieks of rebellion. The greatest innovator in operatic history, Richard Wagner, offers a pertinent lesson in *Meistersinger* on the relationship of rules to rule-breaking, of the old to the new and the new in the old, all drawn from his own rich experience. But even this has not stopped his work from being subjected to a whole catalogue of abuse and misuse, from the Nazis to his most recent exegetes.

Opera has a whole host of conventions, and with good reason. The first is that it tells its stories through music, and this makes the genre subject to the laws of music. It is therefore completely inappropriate to call upon directors from the spoken theatre to 'save' opera from its unnatural 'artificiality'. Opera isn't a natural art form: it is a *musical* art form. Whoever engages with it has to be able to master the music. Opera must not become a play; the play must become music. Another obvious convention is that opera is sung – in other words, it has to take account of the rules of singing. Hanging upside down by your feet or climbing up a precipitous slope is not conducive to singing. People yodel forth only when they reach the summit and have got firm ground underneath their feet. The mouth is a kind of megaphone, situated at the front of the face. So singing an aria upstage, facing away from the audience, is rather pointless. Facing the audience while singing might therefore be considered another useful operatic convention. Yet another is the major role of the orchestra in depicting the characters on stage and in telling the story. For example, the xylophone in Janáček's *Jenůfa* depicts the clattering millwheel, so it doesn't really make much sense when the millwheel is replaced with a computer keyboard. Similarly, if a director interposes pointless stage action at the overwhelming moment in *Fidelio* when the oboe leads up to the words 'O Gott – welch' ein Augenblick', then he can be described only as a musical terrorist.

These examples are unfortunately not invented. And in no way did they originate in any urgent need for new expression. On the contrary: they came from sheer ignorance. Ignorance about the fundamental requirements of the art form, ignorance about its rules, an inability to apply them, and a lack of imagination regarding their possibilities. Ignorance, paired with impotence, is all-too-often celebrated as being 'avant-garde'. People pretend to be revolutionary when in fact they're only barking at the moon. Bertolt Brecht put the record straight when he asked: 'Can we change Shakespeare?' His answer was: 'We can change him if we *can*.' Competence is the basic law of every art. The complex art of opera can be mastered only by competent people who know the story and the musical score inside out and have the same technical and textual ability as a pianist with his fingerings. Only then can one gain the freedom to engage confidently with the actual material, to play with it, to experiment and discover new things. Without this complete mastery of the musical and scenic fundamentals, opera is at the mercy of the amateurism that is so often praised as 'progressive'. Of all the arts, opera has the greatest number of natural enemies among those who practise it. They all have one thing in common: they act without due regard for the music. They practise 'opera without music'. If they did this out of evil intent, it still could amount to something. But no, it's sheer ignorance. At the risk of blasphemy, one is tempted to cry out: 'Father, forgive them, for they know not what they do!'

Nor does this ignorance show any reverence for human greatness. Goethe's insight 'Das Schaudern ist der Menschheit bestes Teil' ('to shudder in awe is the best part of man') means nothing to them. I have often asked myself wherein 'greatness' lies in music. What is it that makes us catch our breath when Beethoven writes something that if written by a lesser man would not move us? Why can Mozart strike us right in our heart when the means he uses are the same as were employed by all his contemporaries? And in an audition on stage, under the pale work lights – I've experienced it a hundred times – how is it that just four bars of Verdi on an out-of-tune piano make everybody stop and listen, even the uninvolved stage hands milling about? What is it that gives music this power over us? I don't know.

But there's one thing I *do* know, and I experience it time and again to my great delight: talent has a feeling for greatness even when it's rebelling against it. It's a sure sign of talent when someone pauses when encountering greatness: they go up to it, begin to study it and assimilate as much of it as possible in order to acquire the tools to go out and do new things of their own, beginning a new game with conventions, breaking old rules or creating new ones, but all the while aware of whose shoulders they're standing on. Only in this way could the mighty edifice of western music be erected by one generation after another: Europe's unique, incomparable gift to the world. Whoever aspires to work in opera should be aware of this.

Useful rules

- ★ Create a precise image of everything you do, say or otherwise express on stage.
- ★ Your imagination must function like a movie in your head.
- ★ First achieve competence, then form an opinion.
- ★ 'Well-meaning' is the opposite of art.
- ★ Play with conventions.
- ★ Know the rules and use them; then question them.
- ★ Break rules where necessary, but with good reason.
- ★ Interesting, innovative, avant-garde, revolutionary or radical are not reasons. At best they can originate in a good reason.
- ★ Tradition is sustainable progress. Link it with innovation.
- ★ Develop a feeling for greatness. It protects against stupidity.

Un ballo in maschera, Giuseppe Verdi, Cologne Opera 1980
Sketch of dancers

The harmony of the spheres

Whoever takes a serious approach to opera will sooner or later come into conflict with opera the institution. There is a vast discrepancy between the aspirations of the works and the institution tasked with presenting them. In the never-ending battle with these inadequacies, one can at least find a little comfort and take courage in being in the very best of company. Hardly had the art of opera been invented when its first-ever grand master, Claudio Monteverdi, was writing letters in which he complained bitterly about the shoddy, negligent treatment meted out to his works. Handel was driven to sickness and financial ruin by the insatiable lust for money of his castrati and prima donnas – not to mention their impossible whims and rivalries. When his star soprano Francesca Cuzzoni one day refused to sing her aria 'Falsa immagine' at a rehearsal of his opera *Ottone*, Handel could take it no longer. He grasped his fractious singer by the waist, cried: 'Oh, Madame, I know you're a veritable she-devil, but I hereby inform you that I am Beelzebub, the lord of all devils', and threatened to drop her out of the window if she made any more objections. The aria was a huge success – and Cuzzoni was still singing it thirty years later when she gave her farewell performance on the London stage.

Gluck's despairing fits of rage during the rehearsals of his works were as talked about and feared in Vienna as they were in Paris. And in his famous letter to court councillor Anton Klein in Mannheim, Mozart despaired of the 'breakdown of German opera' in Vienna: 'It is the greatest misfortune that the directors of both the theatre and the orchestra have been retained, for their ignorance and inactivity have played the greatest part in the failure of their own work. If only a single patriot were on the board – it would all look very different!' In his disappointment, he ends by saying 'after such an outpouring of the heart one should be able to drink oneself drunk without danger of ruining one's health'. But all this is nothing compared to Wagner's lifelong battle with the dragon of the opera institution – a story of crushing defeats and only occasional victories. He described them vividly himself, such as how his run of *Tannhäuser* was cancelled in Paris. As was their wont, the members of the Jockey Club had demanded a ballet in the second act – because they'd still be dining during the first act, and from the third act onwards they would be busy for the rest of the night in the company of the selfsame ladies from the corps de ballet. When Wagner refused to acquiesce to this requirement, the Jockey Club used its influence to ensure that the work was taken from the programme of the Opéra, and didn't even hesitate to cause a riot in the process. Things did not go much better when the first performance of *Tristan* was planned in Vienna. It was cancelled after weeks of rehearsals on account of being 'unplayable'.

When he was Director of the Vienna Opera, Gustav Mahler went into battle against the 'traditions' that he found there, which he called 'Schlamperei' ('shoddiness'). He ruined his health in the process. And so the history of opera continues, via Felsenstein and Strehler down to the present day. And Verdi? At the age of almost eighty he found himself compelled to draw the following, bitter conclusion in a letter to his publisher Giulio Ricordi: 'For my part, I declare that no one has ever, ever, ever succeeded in achieving all the effects that I intended. No one! Never, never!!! Neither singers nor conductors!!!' Thus at the end of these lifelong struggles of the greatest composers, they all had to face the bitter realization that in even the best of circumstances, and despite all their efforts, opera – the depiction of the world through music – can only ever approximate the beautiful ideal embodied in their works.

Must then Verdi's curse be the final word on the matter? No. All the suffering undergone on account of the inadequacies of the institution of opera are balanced out by what actually makes opera unique, irresistible and viable for the future. Because thanks to music it can do something that no other art form can, and which even brings opera in line with the most progressive, modern perceptions of the world: simultaneity in space and time. Every other art form has to choose one partial aspect of the world. A picture, even a vast panorama, is always only an excerpt. Film is a series of images, mostly shots and cutaways, panning and zooming. The camera always has to choose. A statue can be viewed from all sides, but not all at once. One has to move around it in order to see it from another angle. A novel depicts the most rapid of thought processes in a chronological sequence. And even the newest digital and virtual worlds cannot overcome the limitations of time and space.

But music is different – especially opera, because of its concreteness. A simple two-part canon can explain why. 'Frère Jacques, frère Jacques, dormez-vous?' We hear the first voice and the second voice, each on its own and yet simultaneously together. A third, fourth and even a fifth voice can be added to make an ensemble. And yet one still hears each individual voice and all of them together.

In an operatic ensemble, a commentary can also be added to its individual voices – perhaps the first voice is lying and the fourth is angry about it. Or the orchestra can announce that a son with a sword is going to emerge out of the events on stage. To this end it uses a leitmotif that can be combined with other such motifs. And if all this weren't enough, the orchestra can let us hear everything from God's perspective as He looks down on His creatures. In this manner, the subjective view of the characters on stage is combined with an objective perspective from the outside. All this happens so that one hears each thing individually, yet at the same time everything together, in space and time. I know of no other art that can offer such a complete, multi-dimensional image of the world. All other art forms must surely envy opera for this ability. This multi-dimensionality even links opera with the modern scientific worldview that posits the universe itself as being multi-dimensional. The most recent calculations propose the existence of innumerable other universes besides our own, simultaneously emerging and vanishing in many dimensions, so we might actually exist in a multiverse. On a small scale, opera can do this too, and does it every day. Herein lies its potential – especially when one considers the new possibilities opened up by digital technologies and virtual reality. And this potential exists not just in new means of presentation and depiction, but also in form and content, because form and content are always in a mutually stimulating relationship and together can bring forth unimagined innovations.

It might well be that we are standing on the cusp of an age of a new perception of the world, not unlike the new epoch that occurred at the time opera was invented. Back then, Galileo Galilei shattered the crystal bowls of the old Ptolemaic world view with his little essay *Sidereus nuncius* (*Starry messenger*) about Jupiter's moons, and thereby swung open the gates to the vastness of the universe. With the concept of a multiverse, a similar expansion of our horizons might now occur in utterly unimaginable dimensions. Galilei and his successors could still turn their telescopes to the skies to discover unknown galaxies and make them visible, but the notion of a 'multiverse' is impenetrable to us and can reveal itself only in abstract mathematical calculations. I'm therefore inclined to borrow Galilei's title *Sidereus nuncius* and apply it instead to music. For while music has served opera by creating concrete musical depictions of our world, it could then, Pegasus-like, unyoke itself and soar up into its own abstract, ineffable realms and be the new *nuncius* that brings us embassies from those unimaginable worlds. It could perhaps thereby retrieve a concept for us that Johannes Kepler chose as the title of one of his works – *Harmonices mundi* – one that was already dear to the Ancients with their celestial, crystal orbs: the 'harmony of the spheres'. It is this ability of music, namely to take its earthbound effigies and to enhance and amplify them with intimations of eternity, that raises up opera to its true heights where it may then assume its real significance.

Useful rules

- ★ Don't let yourself be discouraged by the inadequacies of the opera institution. You're in the best of company.
- ★ Give your best, even if the result can only approximate to what the work itself demands.
- ★ Opera can do more than other arts. It has a future.

Tristan und Isolde, Richard Wagner, Paris Opera 1985
Designs for Act I, II and III

In place of an epilogue: my teachers

It seems fitting to offer some information about those who educated me in my youth, and to whom my work and my ideas remain indebted to this day.

Max Reinhardt

Reinhardt, naturally, wasn't my teacher – I was only eight years old when he died in exile in the USA. But it wasn't long afterwards that a magical book came into my possession: *Reinhardt and his Stage*, edited by his stage designer Ernst Stern and his dramaturge Heinz Harald. I devoured it, reading it over and over again, and couldn't get enough of it. It described Reinhardt's theatre in all its aspects, as vividly as could be. It explained how a production is developed, retelling all the details of several specific performances. Reinhardt's famous actors were presented to the reader in characteristic roles. Nor was the material aspect of theatre ignored – the revolving stage and other machines, what went on in the workshops, the role assigned to light and music, the make-up artists, the rehearsals with extras, managing the crowd scenes, and even the organization and administration of the whole complex business. And at the end of the book was a chapter entitled 'Twenty-four hours at the Deutsches Theater' that described a single day in Reinhardt's theatre, with sketches by Ernst Stern of the typical, daily activities there. It began at four in the morning with the night watchman and transport deliveries of the backdrops, then proceeded to the dismantling of the old scenery and the erection of the new, then there were the rehearsals, auditions, programme meetings, the bell for the evening performance, the applause and the night-time grind in the workshops until midnight came – the ghosting hour in the empty auditorium. And then, at the close, a picture of the outside façade of the theatre, everything dark except for a light in one window. The caption ran: 'Two in the morning. All is dark; only the administrator is doing his sums.' That was it for me: backdrops, rehearsals, actors, actresses, workshops, auditions, revolving stages and doing sums at night. That's how I wanted to spend my life!

A few weeks later I was already the director of a theatrical troupe, comprised of my siblings and the neighbours' children. We played Max Reinhardt and his theatre, stole bricks and wooden boards (there was nothing else left after the war) and built our stage in the large attic of our parents' house. We wrote plays (one of them even won a prize), we painted backdrops, drilled through walls (much to the horror of our parents) in order to thread through the cables for the lighting equipment, and sewed together all the bedsheets we could get our hands on to create one enormous sheet that would fulfil the Shakespearean stage direction: 'The open sea'. We were also already beating each other up over the money we hadn't yet earned. Since then, little has changed in my life. Only the dimensions have become somewhat more expansive.

Several years later, I had the pleasure of working with some of the actors I knew from that book. They told me all about the glories of Reinhardt's theatre, and whenever they spoke with me it felt like the very first time I'd read that book. One day, I was in Santa Monica in California and stood before the rose-red house in which Reinhardt had lived after emigrating from Germany. It stood right on the edge where the cliffs are being eaten away by the sea. Perhaps the ocean has already swallowed it up. Later, I would be appointed to the Directorate of the Salzburg Festival, where I would spend ten years at the side of Herbert von Karajan, helping to manage and administer the Festival that was Max Reinhardt's great legacy. For me, my journey there possessed its own perfect, innate logic.

Louis Krasner

The violinist Louis Krasner had a huge stroke of luck when Alban Berg wrote him his Violin Concerto 'to the memory of an angel'. Krasner taught at Syracuse University in the USA. I was allowed to join his chamber music class as a cellist, even though I wasn't attending the university, being just sixteen and a high school student on a scholarship programme. But he did a lot more than just let me in: he also made me the cellist of a string quartet whose other members were senior students about to take their final exams. They were several years older than me, and accordingly more advanced. Whether he had some pedagogical plan for me, for I loved to wallow in emotion on my instrument, I do not know. But either way, it was the toughest schooling I ever had to undergo in matters musical. Krasner demanded a huge amount of work and we must have played through half the repertoire for string quartet. Sometimes we also had to broadcast whole quartets at the university's own local radio station – live, without the safety net of recording. I had to cope as well as I could, because otherwise Krasner would say, smiling, 'And here we'll just ignore Michael's cello.' It was in Krasner's lessons that I learnt to think and feel in musical structures, and that I understood how everything has to relate to everything else. But above all I was taught to listen to the others, to react to them and to play my part as something belonging to a bigger whole. These were skills that would later be most useful in the opera. I always regret that opera singers are never put through the rigours of playing quartets as part of their training, for it is probably the most demanding music genre, one in which cheating is impossible. Krasner and the string quartet educated me to be an ensemble player.

Joseph Offenbach

This wasn't just his name: one could also hear it. He came from the town of Offenbach am Main and his Hessian accent remained audible, even in classical roles. Joseph Offenbach was my most important acting teacher. He was a character actor, small in stature and thickset, but with a large head and eyes set wide apart that could almost pop out of their sockets when his enormous imagination was at work. He was able to convey every possible expression, from the deeply demonic to the scurrilous, and the one could slip into the other with alarming ease. Because his repertoire included many smaller roles, he had developed a mastery of precise characterization, and his roles were as sharply defined as a black-and-white silhouette. When he came on stage, any character he was playing was immediately recognizable beyond any doubt.

He managed to teach his students some of this by asking them to imagine everything very precisely. 'If you can't see it, then I can't see it either.' For example, he compelled me to draw the room in which a scene was playing. 'Is there perhaps a fly on the wall?' he asked. Then he taught me to develop a character systematically, with a certain degree of mistrust. He hated nothing more than imprecision – he called it 'Geschlabbel' ('slobbering'). The situation, condition, character and intentions of a figure had to be made clearly recognizable before he allowed an actor to expose it to emotion. One can still admire his art of characterization in his many films, which are regularly shown on German TV. For me, he was the ideal imagination trainer.

Fritz Kortner

Kortner was rehearsing Shakespeare's *Twelfth Night* at the Kammerspiele in Munich. His legendary reputation had preceded him, as he was the subject of innumerable anecdotes. He was said to be extremely difficult: excessive in his demands and insatiable in what he required of his actors. We acting students from the Otto Falckenberg School quickly found out that this was our chance to witness a mighty volcano in full eruption. But how? His rehearsals were kept strictly closed to outsiders. Any intruder would risk being caught in the red-hot lava. All the same, we crept into the auditorium in the dark, hiding on the ground behind the last rows of the stalls in order to get a picture of Vesuvius at work. But a treacherous assistant betrayed us. The lights went on, and we were found out. Kortner went into a rage. There was even talk of getting us expelled from theatre school. We had to file up to see the intendant, Hans Schweikart. He was a wise man, and after giving us a stern look he warned that we shouldn't let ourselves get caught the next time, otherwise we'd get him into real trouble. Irresistibly drawn back to the scene of our crime by the glimpses we'd seen, two fellow students and I decided to risk it once again. We managed to get into a projection booth that afforded our expeditions a relative degree of safety. And the risk was worth it. Because what now unfolded before our eyes and ears, hour after hour, was a miracle of imagination, skill and intensity, all manifesting itself in a personality of titanic, biblical proportions.

It was here I learnt that there are almost unlimited possibilities for playing a character or a scene. Kortner started a scene and rehearsed it for a long time until it began to run smoothly, only to cast everything overboard and start again, completely differently. This might be repeated several times until the actors were exhausted. Some of them then claimed Kortner didn't know what he wanted. His angry answer was: in life, like on stage, you can *never* really know what you want. His exuberant imagination compelled him to try out many different possibilities. So he was always short of time and never finished. His obsession with maximum expression knew no boundaries and he drove his actors into all the depths and heights of their own existence. He expected too much of everyone around him. Often too much of the audience as well. Of the many productions of his that I was able to see, a frequent criticism was that they were too long-winded in their obsession with details, too unwieldy and thus too exhausting. I always found them too short. I could have watched many more hours of this mighty stream of imagination and life, which impressed me so deeply that even today, almost sixty years later, I could play through whole scenes from memory. Above all, it was thanks to Kortner that I grasped that there is basically no difference between life and theatre.

Leopold Lindtberg

In many respects, Leopold Lindtberg was the opposite of Kortner, even though he too came from Vienna and, like him, had grown up in the old imperial era of Austrian culture. His sparkling, sanguine temperament was paired with a sharp, analytical mind and a keen, vibrant sensuality. And on top of this he possessed a talent for mimicry that came straight from the tradition of Viennese popular theatre. Alfred Kerr, the redoubtable critic in the era of the Weimar Republic, once wrote: 'Leopold Lindtberg – name of honour!'

Lindtberg's credo was this: 'A stage director has always had only one purpose, namely to allow the drama and the actors playing it to flourish. A performance that speaks directly through itself, without any obtrusive ideas or concepts to draw attention to the director, is his biggest compliment. It seems to me that the best director is he who, when his work is done, allows the naturalness and the conviction of the performance to make him invisible.'

Lindtberg was famous for his performances of the classics, which he often staged in large-scale cycles. But he was just as much a born director for comedies. His temperament, his musicality, his sense of colour, form and rhythm and his infallible feeling for a punchline made him predestined to direct comedy – which is a demanding genre and, strictly speaking, even more difficult than tragedy. In contrast to Kortner, he had a sure sense of what I like to call the overarching rhythm of an evening at the theatre – that arc of tension that keeps the audience on tenterhooks from the beginning to the end. Lindtberg profited here from his experience in film, in which even more than in the theatre the overall effect is dependent on the rhythm, structure, tempo and format of a sequence of images. Forced into exile by the Nazis, he almost single-handedly created the Swiss film industry, under the most difficult circumstances. He enjoyed several worldwide successes with his films, one of which even won an Oscar for original screenplay.

I was Lindtberg's assistant for his legendary production of both parts of Goethe's *Faust* at the Salzburg Festival. Almost all the major actors and actresses in German theatre were involved in it, down to the smallest roles, and I was afterwards responsible for the production for three years. It was something of a leap of faith on his part when he appointed me his deputy when he became the director of the renowned Zurich Schauspielhaus, for I was just thirty at the time, and he assigned me full authority over matters of planning. All the greatest and best actors and actresses of twentieth-century German theatre went through the doors of the Schauspielhaus at that time. Depending on the work being performed and the cast it needed, there were often between five and ten big stars on stage. And I was able to work with them as their director, as well as with major authors such as Max Frisch, Friedrich Dürrenmatt and Arthur Miller.

'The greatest sin that can be committed in our profession is to assume that the members of the audience – our fellow human beings – are stupid. Only when our hearts and minds can offer them the best and the cleverest will it be good enough for a good audience.' This maxim, like so much else, is something I owe to Leopold Lindtberg.

Caspar Neher

'When our friend makes his sketches, his starting point is always "the people" and "what happens to and through them" ... almost everything else that belongs to the profession of the stage designer – things aesthetic and stylistic – he does with his little finger.' Thus wrote Brecht in his 'Speech by the playwright about the theatre of the stage builder Caspar Neher', a friend from his youth and a fellow traveller on his way to worldwide fame. And that also describes the Neher I got to know at the Zurich Schauspielhaus. But he wasn't just a set designer. He was much, much more: a poet and librettist for half a dozen operas by Kurt Weill and Rudolf Wagner-Régeny, a painter, an architect, a dramaturge and – when necessary – a stage director too. He was the most all-encompassing man of the theatre I have ever encountered.

I have no idea what moved him to take me under his wing. But he did it emphatically and didn't go easy on me. Above all, he taught me to ask questions – questions as if I were a 'man from Mars' who'd just fallen to Earth and had what Brecht termed an 'alien view' of things and relationships, seeing them as if they were quite new and had never been seen before. That was often very exhausting. He also taught me to work with materials in a technical, practical sense. What's warm, what's cold, and what is suited to which play. Although time was in short supply, he patiently waited while I did the lighting for his stage set, only to ask at the end, politely, whether I found my 'wishy-washy' results beautiful? He then scrapped everything I'd done and gave me a masterly lesson in how a direct light has a single source and thus a single direction, whereas diffuse light arises from being reflected. Most of all, he insisted on doing what was technically practicable and, wherever feasible, he wanted it done in the simplest possible way. And even more importantly: what can we omit? What does the audience know, or what can it work out for itself so it doesn't have to be shown? Only what was necessary and had a role in the drama should have a place on the stage. Everything had to serve the actors.

He loved opera, and he introduced a dash of Brechtian soberness to it, trying to drive out everything that was pompous and overblown – as if laying it out to dry. And the results were splendid. In his hands, opera attained a clear structure that was related directly to the music, which I found particularly appealing. Regrettably, our acquaintance lasted only two years before it ended with Caspar Neher's death. But he taught me much in that time. Since then, the set designer's workshop has been one of my favourite places in a theatre, a place where the spiritual is united with the material and the one has to hold its ground against the other. Caspar Neher had mastered this alchemy like no one else.

Walter Felsenstein

After my aforementioned conversion to opera thanks to Walter Felsenstein I began to acquaint myself with his working methods. He believed in opera as music theatre, 'with equal emphasis on both these words', as he said. My entrance into this world was made easier because his former stage designer, the brilliant Rudolf Heinrich, had moved to the West and had become a close friend and colleague of mine. With his help, everything that I learnt about opera I was able to try out and realize on stage. I also visited the Komische Oper in East Berlin as often as I could to admire Felsenstein's famous productions. He had developed the high art of letting the music seem to emerge spontaneously out of the action on stage. This was naturally possible only because he had tailored the action precisely to the music. Along with his subtle musico-dramaturgical analysis of the works, this interplay was what really impressed me. He also rehearsed for an unusually long time. When a journalist once asked him if it was true that he always needed nine months for a production he was highly indignant. That was slanderous, he said – he could also do it in just six.

I got to know Felsenstein personally when I was a young intendant at the Mannheim National Theatre. In this house, rich in tradition, I now declared that we would in future perform operas on the basis of Felsenstein's principles and working methods. He was clearly pleased by this, because from then on he took an active interest in my work and the work of my theatre. We engaged in a lively dialogue, and my first *Falstaff* and a series of Mozart productions with the brothers Rudolf and Reinhard Heinrich (Reinhard was Felsenstein's head of costumes) was the subject of intense, at times controversial debate because I didn't agree with him in everything. His demand that a singer should reach a state of mind and body in which singing was his only option seemed to me too exalted, because music and singing are basically just a convention – an agreement about the means of expression to be employed in opera. I suspected that his demand was merely a cleverly contrived working hypothesis designed to get singers into the condition of the character they have to portray – something they otherwise often prefer to ignore. But he vehemently denied that. No, he was wholly serious about it. I, in contrast, believed that the actor's ability to create reality through his imagination is also wholly sufficient for the music-actor.

How often does one get the opportunity to debate such issues with a great master of the profession? What he taught me – and a whole generation of theatre people with me – was to take opera completely seriously, and to underlay it with a reality in order for music to be justified through the action and the action through the music. In other words, to conceive opera as a great dramatic genre. In this, he can remain a role model to this day.

Giorgio Strehler

I saw Giorgio Strehler's world-famous production of Goldoni's *Arlecchino, Servant of Two Masters* as a student in a guest performance in Munich. The next day, Strehler even came himself to our seminar at the university, together with several of his superb actors. After that, I was so addicted to him that for a while my own work ran the risk of imitating him. A critic later once described me as 'a German Protestant with a yearning for the south that no set designer can fulfil for him'. That was a good observation, and well put. But this yearning found fulfilment in Strehler's productions. The Piccolo Teatro di Milano in the Via Rovello – a former cinema hall below street level – became my place of pilgrimage. Everything that I had dreamed theatre could be was realized there. Both form and content were realized with skill, precision, elegance and ease. Everything followed a particular rhythm and played masterfully with tension and release in a way that was almost musical. The light and the atmosphere were magical, yet without losing their reality. All this took place in a small space with a tiny stage that was neither very broad nor deep, and had no special technical equipment. As a result, everything retained a human dimension that was focused on the body of the actor. If Wagner praised himself as a 'master of transition' in music, Strehler was his equal on stage.

Perhaps it was a stroke of luck on Strehler's part that his decades-long desire for a bigger, better equipped theatre was realized only late in his career. In his small-scale empire of the Piccolo Teatro, his flamboyant and often capricious manner, reminiscent of a Baroque *principe*, was economically viable and justified by his magnificent results. If ever the old adage about true mastery proving itself in limitation applied, then it was here – albeit involuntarily. In the opera house, with its ponderous apparatus, Strehler still achieved grandiose things. But, as he himself admitted, it was more difficult for him. He was born very musical, and assumed that his singers had as much theatre craft as he did. So he became impatient and irritable when their acting was clumsy. And this was reflected in the results. If he was unsurpassable in the spoken theatre, one could still try to match him in opera.

Our personal relationship was limited to just a few businesslike encounters. When I was at the Zurich Schauspielhaus, I tried to ensure that the Piccolo Teatro came to give regular guest performances of Strehler productions. Later, when I was in the Directorate in Salzburg, I was told he was upset about not being invited back to the Festival. Of course I had tried hard to get him again. But after a half-finished, near-failed production of *The Magic Flute* with Karajan, nothing more could be done in his favour, something I deeply regretted. But in my work he was and remains ever present. I have endeavoured to unite Felsenstein's stern realism with Strehler's formal elegance. Together with the wonderful stage designer Mauro Pagano, who died far, far too soon, I think that we sometimes managed to achieve it.

Friedrich Dürrenmatt

I got to know Friedrich Dürrenmatt at the Zurich Schauspielhaus, during the rehearsals for the world première of his bitter comedy *The Physicists*. Before this I had produced several plays by the Viennese playwright Nestroy in Switzerland. This seemed to please Dürrenmatt, for he always regarded Nestroy as a kindred spirit. When I was put in charge of planning for the Schauspielhaus, there were meetings for performances of other plays by Dürrenmatt, and these occasionally took place in his house high above the Lake of Neuchâtel. After work was done, all kinds of hijinks could ensue. Here I should perhaps add that clowning around can be thoroughly conducive to an artistic collaboration. It helps people to relax and is usually a sign that they understand each other. I'm almost tempted to add another rule to all those mentioned above: 'Clowning around helps.' With Dürrenmatt and me, it turned out that we were both railway timetable addicts – people who love reading timetables as a means of stimulating their imagination. Regrettably, this is a dying species because the Internet has made railway timetable books almost extinct. But Dürrenmatt had a whole collection of them at home, so while drinking an excellent red wine we would fight it out over who could find the quickest connection from Niederbipp to Vladivostok (Niederbipp not being an invention of Dürrenmatt's but a tiny town, together with Oberbipp, in the canton of Bern). Dürrenmatt won. Later, when I was the intendant at the Mannheim National Theatre, I invited him to direct his play *The Collaborator*, which he did with aplomb and to the delight of everyone involved – actors and audience alike. And we indulged in similar competitions, sometimes along with his friend the composer Gottfried von Einem. I got the impression that this pastime served to release Dürrenmatt from the burden of his unfathomable intelligence, which he endeavoured to hide behind the mask of a ponderous, mischievous jester.

Dürrenmatt had an instinctive knack of thinking in dramatic constellations and in opposing scenarios. He felt that only comedy was able to cope with the horrors of the world. His understanding of the theatre was as phenomenal as his feeling for the absurd and for punchlines. 'You can't play meaning, it has to emerge from the action.' And: 'The quality of theatre depends on the height of your viewpoint for looking out on the world.' Those were his maxims. And he always insisted that we shouldn't fear fate, but chance. This was because his true realm, where he really belonged, was the daemonic, and he opened my eyes to it. The fact that some of my best work in later years also belonged to that realm – such as Offenbach's *Tales of Hoffmann*, Strindberg's *Dance of Death*, Britten's *The Turn of the Screw* and Henze's *We Come to the River* – is something I owe to Dürrenmatt.

■ ■ ■

I ought to mention many more here from whom I have learnt. Such as Jean-Louis Barrault, who played the pantomime Baptiste in the film *Les enfants du paradis*, which I watched over and over again when I was a teenager, and which left a lasting impression on me. I even met Barrault once in New York, during the year I spent at school in the USA. Or the two major architects Richard Neutra and Jørn Utzon. Utzon had designed the Sydney Opera House, and I worked for a long time with him on designs for a new Schauspielhaus in Zurich. Had it been realized, Switzerland would today possess an architectural landmark to match Australia's icon.

I owe my thanks to all those I have mentioned, and to the many who have here remained nameless. My aim now is to be a catalyst between the generations: taking what I was allowed to learn from those before me, and passing it on to the young in whom my hopes reside.

APPENDIX 1

All the 'useful rules' in overview, for those who make opera

What is opera?

- ★ Opera: enacting a story through music.
- ★ Understand the difference between music, and music for a purpose.
- ★ Define the purpose of the music.
- ★ Become a 'music detective'.
- ★ Know the orchestra.
- ★ Give the orchestra a reason to play.
- ★ Train your imagination.

The heart

- ★ Go straight to the heart.

The seven 'W's

- ★ Start with the six 'W's: **W**ho? **W**here? **W**hen? **W**hat? ho**W**? **W**hy?
- ★ Then define the seventh: **W**hom? – the addressee.
- ★ Locate the addressee.
- ★ Change the addressee where necessary.
- ★ If the addressee is imaginary, choose a fixed point and address it instead.

Sense and sensuality

- ★ Find out: what does the work mean?
- ★ Consider: what does your role contribute to it?
- ★ Make sense. Both in the details and in the overall context.
- ★ Sense trumps effect.

Bodies in space

- ★ The body in the space is already part of the action.
- ★ Develop a feeling for space in relation to your co-performers.
- ★ Sameness is boring. Be dissimilar.
- ★ The singer stands further upstage, the listener further downstage.
- ★ Position yourself according to the golden section, not in the centre.
- ★ A king can't play himself. Those surrounding him play him.
- ★ Stand at an angle to the stage ramp, not in the 'pancake position'.
- ★ Maintain your relationship with your partner. Avoid the 'tenor's turn'.
- ★ Seek a position between two fronts. It's dramatically effective.
- ★ Wherever possible, place the leading voice in an ensemble on the left.
- ★ Leave space around you. Otherwise objects can become competitors.
- ★ Hold your stance – don't wobble around.

- ★ When you move, make sure it's with a purpose and a specific goal.
- ★ Violence and torture have a greater impact on a live body on stage than in the two-dimensional images of film and TV.
- ★ Fill the space with breath. If the audience coughs, you've got too little breath.
- ★ Regard sentences and musical phrases as the arch of a bridge. Make sure to reach the other side.
- ★ Master the play of tension and release.

Movement

- ★ No soul without a body.
- ★ Bodily expression precedes speech and music through the 'upbeat' of the breath.
- ★ Movement starts at the centre, the solar plexus.
- ★ Emotions rise up from the solar plexus to consciousness.
- ★ 'Act from your guts'.
- ★ Observe the movements of animals and learn from them.
- ★ Train your body as a musical instrument, just as you train your voice.
- ★ The order of practising is: difficult – normal – easy – beautiful (Stanislavski).
- ★ Gestures must be plastic and readable, otherwise they are useless.
- ★ One clear, cleanly executed gesture is better than five small, quick ones.

- ★ Underlay gestures with 'baby text' in order to make them more readable.
- ★ Direct gestures towards the focal point.
- ★ Fumbling is the death of both theatre and music.
- ★ The eye spontaneously follows movement.
- ★ Determine when to split musical and physical expression.
- ★ The body can do only one thing at a time; music can do many things.
- ★ The body and the breath can oscillate rapidly between different states of being.
- ★ In ensembles, individual movement must be coordinated with the music.
- ★ When actions and movements go against the music, make sure they are in counterpoint with it.
- ★ Movements begin with an 'upbeat' in the opposite direction.
- ★ Find the rhythm of movements like circus artists.
- ★ Link activities to the music. Sectionalize actions and match them with single musical phrases.
- ★ Don't bow forwards unless you're a servant or when you lose control.
- ★ 'Épauler' – hold your bearing.
- ★ Happiness takes wing, unhappiness weighs down.
- ★ A cry always goes upwards.
- ★ Be insistent; don't give up too soon.
- ★ Duels are focused through the eyes.

- ★ Don't be afraid of pathos. But the emotion must be bigger than the gesture.
- ★ Big feeling demands big breath.
- ★ Create a 'movement score' that matches the musical score.

Le physique du rôle

- ★ 'Le physique du rôle' is a decisive criterion.
- ★ Study and utilize the physical gestures of different languages.
- ★ Give a character the gestures of his or her social status.
- ★ Study good cartoons.
- ★ Only what has breath and an upbeat belongs in music theatre.

Discomfort and inconvenience

- ★ The comfortable is the enemy of expression. The uncomfortable is more expressive.
- ★ Incorporate obstacles in a performance. They increase tension and interest.
- ★ Use props as obstacles.
- ★ Develop slapstick scenes (where appropriate), using obstacles.

Bank robbers

- ★ Conspirators act under tension, but inconspicuously.
- ★ Prepare your evil deed with few slow movements and with bated breath.

★ Mishaps can increase the tension.

★ When in a hiding place, play out the tension of listening and the danger of discovery – otherwise the audience won't believe you're in hiding.

★ Speak 'asides' behind the 'wall' of your own shoulder and/or combined with an action.

Pretend theatre

★ Don't pretend to do or feel something. Just do or feel it.

★ Merge expression and technique into the unity of body and voice.

★ Don't mistake forcing for intensity.

★ Imagination is better than hysteria to reach a high emotional level.

★ Sing on the breath, not on your vocal cords.

The 'trizophrenic' upbeat

★ Be ahead of the music and 'switch' in good time.

★ Lagging behind the music is unintentionally comic.

★ '*And* – !' is the magic formula for the upbeat, for both the music and the action on stage.

★ Decide which is the more important: either 'don't phone ahead', or 'take a big swing to slap hard'.

★ Train Karajan's 'trizophrenia': cue, control and preparation, all at the same time.

The complete music-actor

- ★ 'Masticare le parole' – chew the words until they are completely comprehensible.
- ★ Practice your lines out loud, with a cork clenched between your teeth.
- ★ Look for the two words in a sentence that are vital for its meaning. Make sure they are understood by everyone in the auditorium.
- ★ Your role is how you place your feet.

Mozart

- ★ Take Mozart as your teacher. What you learn from him can be applied everywhere.
- ★ 'Mozart is a brain problem'. Train your 'switching speed' in Mozart.
- ★ Learn the 'micro-management' of music.
- ★ Play ping-pong! – action and reaction – with partners, orchestra and audience.
- ★ Determine how, in an ensemble, the ball is passed musically from one performer to the next.
- ★ Determine the emotional climax of an aria. Then shape it accordingly.
- ★ Define the social position of your character.
- ★ Servants and subordinates work.
- ★ Play every character as intelligently as possible.
- ★ Assume that the audience is intelligent, too.

- ★ Pay attention to the 'physiology' in Mozart's music, and adapt to it.
- ★ Choose the dramatically most effective version when playing a character.
- ★ Be fair; show all sides of a character and let the audience make its own judgement.
- ★ Include the opposite in your performance. Show that a scene could actually have a different outcome.
- ★ If the music doesn't take sides, let it keep its secrets.

Recitative

- ★ The (secco) recitative is important and must be worked out carefully.
- ★ Recitatives must be comprehensible. 'Parlare intonato!'
- ★ Find the reason behind the text and the music.
- ★ The sequence: thinking – breathing – speaking always applies.
- ★ Have an idea of where the people and things are that you're talking about.
- ★ Investigate and develop the biography of a character.
- ★ Define what happens 'behind the scenes' in between the appearances of a character.
- ★ 'Listening pays half the rent'.
- ★ Use the 'Huh?' and '*What*?!' techniques.
- ★ Practise double-takes.
- ★ Link the recitative to an activity. Use props.

- ★ 'Activity leads to the truth of a character'.
- ★ Use the technique of interruption.
- ★ Let punchlines drop casually like a ripe apple from a tree.
- ★ Don't ruin punchlines by fumbling and fidgeting.
- ★ Don't aim for laughs.
- ★ Make full use of the freedom a recitative allows – to expand, accelerate, add colour, illustrate, rhythmize, imitate or pause. Develop your imagination as a 'recitative composer'.
- ★ Learn the difference between pause and hole. Play with the pauses.
- ★ If you find a text difficult, say or sing it in your native dialect.
- ★ When addressing the audience, play 'cat-and-mouse' with them.
- ★ Put a high value on the transition from a recitative to an aria. Don't let there be a hole.

Being comic

- ★ Comedy is more difficult than tragedy.
- ★ Play comedies seriously.
- ★ Incorporate the possibility of tragedy when performing comedy.
- ★ Never sacrifice the truth of a character for a laugh.
- ★ Let the laughs look after themselves.
- ★ Never subvert your character.
- ★ Play with opposites, such as big/small, slow/quick, pathetic/banal.

- ★ Don't instruct the audience when to laugh.

'Too many notes ...'

- ★ Determine what the music says, and what the stage action says.
- ★ When must you show something, and when can you let the music show it?
- ★ When is the performer a slave of the orchestra? And when is the music a servant of the action?
- ★ What can be left out because the audience knows it anyway?

Dramaturgy

- ★ The basic question is: what is to be said, and how, so it might be understood?
- ★ The basic prerequisite is: a precise knowledge of the libretto and the score.
- ★ Tools: use everything that helps you to understand the work.
- ★ Read the work from a contemporary perspective, and interpret it on its own inherent terms.
- ★ Play for the audience, not for insiders, critics or the media.
- ★ The basis of understanding is: who wants what from whom, and why?
- ★ If you adapt a work, label it honestly.
- ★ 'Modern' is decided in the auditorium.
- ★ Don't make claims about things you don't understand. If you *do* want to understand them, go and learn about them.

- ★ A major change to the story implies a change to the music. Action and music must depend on each other.
- ★ Understanding music's structure increases music's emotional power.
- ★ Definitions: good – bad, right – wrong; interesting – boring, truth – lies.
- ★ Create the 'drop height' and emphasize contrasts.
- ★ Heroes are people who can't really do what they end up doing. They are weak and have to overcome their fears.
- ★ Truth and clarity come first. Style and aesthetics are a result of them.
- ★ Find out where the composer and his work can be helped.
- ★ Practise dramaturgical thinking. It takes time and patience.
- ★ The work is the star. Everyone else is a servant.

Breaking the rules

- ★ Create a precise image of everything you do, say or otherwise express on stage.
- ★ Your imagination must function like a movie in your head.
- ★ First achieve competence, then form an opinion.
- ★ 'Well-meaning' is the opposite of art.
- ★ Play with conventions.
- ★ Know the rules and use them; then question them.
- ★ Break rules where necessary, but with good reason.
- ★ Interesting, innovative, avant-garde, revolutionary or radical are not reasons. At best they can originate in a good reason.

- ★ Tradition is sustainable progress. Link it with innovation.
- ★ Develop a feeling for greatness. It protects against stupidity.

The harmony of the spheres

- ★ Don't let yourself be discouraged by the inadequacies of the opera institution. You're in the best of company.
- ★ Give your best, even if the result can only approximate to what the work itself demands.
- ★ Opera can do more than other arts. It has a future.

APPENDIX 2

A masterclass in opera, for those who love it or hate it

It is somewhat unusual in literature to repeat the whole content of a book again at the close. This appendix, however, is not meant to be literature. Instead, the content of this book is here offered in the form of a theatrical text, as a masterclass for the audience in the 'crafty art of opera' – whose fullest effect can be felt only on the stage itself.

I have presented this kind of masterclass in many different countries and in several different languages to audiences that loved opera, but understood little of it and were keen to know more. They reacted everywhere with utter delight. So perhaps this is also a way to turn opera-haters into opera-lovers.

My purpose in presenting this masterclass in written form is to prompt as many theatres as possible to stage it. Opera lovers (and haters) can also follow the below text while listening to a good recording of *Figaro* – preferably accompanied by a glass of fine red wine.

Introduction: *Figaro*, Overture

Hampe [rushes in, interrupting the music]: Stop! ... hold on please ... stop!!! I'm quite out of breath. *Why?* Because we're in a crazy day – *La folle journée, Le marriage de Figaro*, we're at Figaro's wedding where all events come tumbling one after another. So it's impossible to keep up with them.

As you've no doubt heard, opera means telling a story in music – no, not 'telling', 'enacting'. 'Favola per musica' or 'dramma per musica' – a 'tale for music' or 'drama for music' – were the names of this new art form when it emerged in Florence 400 years ago. So let's first see how Mozart depicts this 'crazy day' in music, right at the start of the overture. For that, however, I need your help. You have to count the measures – don't worry, it won't be more than ten, and you can use your fingers to help you. Yes, you can! So let's go. [Music]

One, two, three, four, five, six, seven, eight ... stop! You see, eight measures. That's what we call a regular eight-measure period. Every respectable composer writes them, and this one, naturally, is very fast – *presto*. Like I said, you can barely keep up with it ... *What's that? There's something wrong*? Did anyone notice anything? The orchestra (our pianist) has played a trick on you, for he played the first measure – *diddle-diddle-dim* – twice [music]. So we have to count again. Fingers at the ready! [to the musician]: *And play it properly this time!* One, two, three, four, five, six, seven ... oops! Just where we would expect the eighth measure of the regular period, Mozart is already in the first measure of the next period. You see: that's why I'm out of breath.

Now that we've got an inkling of how an event can be expressed through music, we can carry on with our opera. Well, no, we can't just yet! If we were in a concert, we could; but not in opera. *Why not?* Because in a concert we play music, whereas in an opera we play music for a purpose. Where is the difference?

It's very simple. In Beethoven's Fifth Symphony, the opening – *ta-ta-ta-taaa* 

expresses and means: *ta-ta-ta-taaa* and nothing else. This music doesn't signify anything outside itself. This is absolute music. Extremely, intensely expressive music, but it's abstract. It's the musical material that Beethoven uses to create the grandiose first movement of his symphony.

[Hampe sings; music.] 'Zu Hilfe, zu Hilfe, sonst bin ich verloren, der listigen Schlange zum Opfer erkoren!' ('Help, oh help, or else I'm lost, doomed to be a victim of this cruel serpent') – this scurrying, scudding, pulsating opening to the first scene of Mozart's *Magic Flute*, with its snake-like bass writhing upwards [music], is something very different. Here the music is expressing very concrete things, namely, the specific panic felt by this specific Prince Tamino in a specific situation and in a specific state of mind.

Music – the most abstract of the arts – is here married to the dramatic arts in order to express something quite concrete. Music is being used for a purpose. Purists might even say: abused.

That's why we can't yet proceed with our opera. First, we have to determine the purpose of its music. For this, I'd like to ask the singers of Figaro and Susanna to come to me [both come forward]. Now let me ask the following. *Who are you?*

[The following proceeds as a dialogue:]

- ▷ A servant of the Count.
- ▷ The maid of the Countess.

Ah, so you both belong to the palace servants. And *where* are you?

- ▷ In an unused connecting room.
- ▷ On the right, it leads to the Countess's chambers.
- ▷ And on the left it leads to the Count's chambers.

When are you here together?

- ▷ Early in the morning ...
- ▷ before our work begins for the day.

And *what* are you doing?

- ▷ I'm furnishing the empty room.
- ▷ I've arrived by chance and don't know what he's doing until he explains it to me.

And *how* are you doing this?

- ▷ I'm measuring the room to determine how best to put up the splendid bed that the Count has given us as a gift.
- ▷ I'm showing him my bridal veil that I've spent half the night sewing.

And *why* are you doing all of this?

- ▷ [both] Because today's our wedding day.

So now we know quite a few things about the two of them – things the music is meant to express. We've found this out through the method of the seven 'W's that we are wise to follow: **W**ho? **W**here? **W**hen? **W**hat? ho**W**? and **W**hy? Who am I? Where am I? When am I? What am I doing or what is it I want to do? hoW am I doing it? And above all: Why am I doing this? And now comes the seventh, final 'W': **W**hom am I addressing? All of this doesn't yet describe in full the persons depicted in the music, but it offers us a kind of profiling – like the police do when they're hunting for a criminal as yet unknown to them. Now we have this information, we can finally get started.

[There follow the first duet, recitative and second duet from *The Marriage of Figaro*.]

You have surely noticed how the music expresses things here; for example, how it depicts the man and the woman right at the beginning. There is a rather stubborn, dry theme that depicts Figaro [music], which is quite typical of men when they're concentrating on their work. And then – what a contrast – we hear the tender, feminine oboe when Susanna appears [music]. And, at the end, we can hear how the high spirits of the opening peter out on account of their problems with the Count.

But how can we find out what the music is actually *telling* us? For this, all those involved – the singers, the director, even the conductor – have to become 'music detectives'. And what does a 'music detective' do? Exactly what a police detective does. [Hampe demonstrates.] He discovers a dead body, a man obviously killed by a stab wound. The knife, however, is nowhere to be found. But then our police detective discovers a drop of blood on the ground, then another and yet another, all leading towards the exit. These clues allow him to deduce that the murderer carried out the knife dripping with blood. In other words, he can draw conclusions about the whole event that took place here. And this is precisely what the music detective does. [Music: short examples.] Here there's a change in the orchestration and the clarinet enters; there we find a harmonic modulation or a dynamic shift, then a change in tempo. These, so to speak, are the drops of blood for the music detective. They allow him to draw conclusions about the whole event as the composer imagined it when he wrote his music. And now the performers have to embody and enact this scene, in accordance with the composer's score.

In this context, however, there is another question. *What* is the orchestra? When I ask this, I usually get a mumbled answer: *Well, the orchestra is simply there and it plays.* That's certainly what it does. But *what* is it? I tell the singers this: the orchestra is *you*! It expresses what is happening inside the person who's on stage: his character, his situation, his state of mind, his actions and reactions and many other things too. *You* are the orchestra. That's why you, the singers, have to know the orchestra and what happens in it. Of course, the orchestra is a lot more besides. It can comment on what's happening, it can create atmosphere, and it can set up relationships and embody meaning through the use of leitmotifs. But all the same, the first, most important function of the orchestra is to depict the characters on stage. Conversely, they have to know the orchestra and take their cues from it, even when they have to think exactly the opposite of what they sing, as in the duet between Susanna and Marcellina: two women joined in mutual hatred who shower each other with poisoned compliments.

[There follows the duet between Susanna and Marcellina from *The Marriage of Figaro*.]

The orchestra expresses what is happening in the minds and hearts of the characters. But if you have paid careful attention, you'll have noticed that the singers turn things on their head, for it seems as if *they* create the music, and the orchestra is in fact reacting to what they are singing. That's how it should be. The singer has to give the orchestra a good reason to play what it does. The singer first has to get excited before the orchestra can play his excitement. If the singer doesn't do this – or does it too late – then the orchestra has no reason for its agitation. The singer must always be a little ahead of the music. This, by the way, is also how it is in everyday life. Before you say something to me you have to do two things: think and breathe. Otherwise you simply cannot say anything. Only when the singer succeeds in convincing you that he is creating the music out of the very moment, then you'll say: 'He's good, he's believable!', even though you all know that in fact it was Mozart who wrote the music, over two hundred years ago.

And what makes you believe him? What is it that lets you empathize with the performer, to cry with him, or to laugh with him? People always say it's the voice of the singer. In fact, it's really the *sound* of his voice. When a violinist plays a concerto, you're not interested in his fiddle, but in the sound he creates with it. This is how it is in opera, too. The voice is the instrument. Only the actual sound it makes touches you and awakens your interest in the character and the events on stage.

So what exactly *is* this 'sound'? Here's my succinct definition: air + idea = sound. The singer releases air from his body and this air is transformed into a tone by his vocal cords. This tone then encounters the 'idea', namely imagination: being sad or happy, angry or in love. A sad voice sounds completely different from a happy one, and everybody hears immediately whether someone is in love or aggressive. So it is the breath, transformed into a tone, which meets imagination, thus creating the vocal sound. Pay attention to this in the following trio:

[There follows the Trio from the first act of *The Marriage of Figaro*.]

So it is the 'idea' that creates sound. And here we have reached the quintessence of all theatre: imagination. The imagination of poets and composers, the imagination of performers and, last but not least, the imagination of the audience: *your* imagination. If you have trained your imagination – oh yes, you can indeed train it, just like you can exercise your biceps – then your trained imagination will immediately translate everything into an image, into a reality governed by the law of the 'magic if' – 'if it were like that …'. Every child can create its own reality with imagination. A piece of wood becomes a spaceship with which it can navigate the universe; in the next moment, the spaceship becomes a light sabre when the child imagines itself a Jedi warrior from *Star Wars*; and then the piece of wood is transformed again, into a ship, and the child becomes a Pirate of the Caribbean. When his mother calls him, she remains unheard because the child is so immersed in the reality created by his imagination. Imagination is the primary condition of all performing arts, here on stage and down in the auditorium.

So it is imagination that through the breath determines the sound of the voice. Some indigenous peoples have only one word for both 'breath' and 'soul'. Perfectly plausible. Because if we have no breath, we have no soul. Breath is the soul's means of transport – for it is ultimately the performer's soul that is transferred to you, the audience. Our breath controls both our body and our voice.

The body was the first-ever instrument. It existed millions of years before the voice evolved. The ichthyosaurus could express itself unmistakably through its body, signalling 'go away or I'll eat you'. The voice only came much later. But from then on, voice and body belonged together. In opera, they form a unity of vocal sound and bodily expression, driven jointly by our breath (or, if you prefer: by our soul) with the goal of embodying music. Wagner called this 'visible deeds of music'. Now look and listen for them in the following aria of Figaro, with its highly complex network of relationships.

[There follows Figaro's aria 'Non piu andrai' at the close of the first act of *The Marriage of Figaro*.]

Now you have already got to know some of the basic elements of opera. Opera means depicting a story through music; opera music is not just music, but music for a purpose; and in order to find out what that purpose is, you have to become a 'music detective'. You have learnt to apply the seven 'W' questions, you have pondered what the orchestra is and how sound is created, and you have heard something about the all-encompassing role of imagination. You're almost experts already! Almost – but not quite. Because knowledge isn't yet art. Art first has to be made, and for that you need techniques and rules. The problem is, however, that techniques and rules are largely unknown in opera. For example: every expression, whether from man or beast, has an addressee. People speak to each other, to themselves, to God, or to an idea of someone or something. Every prayer is directed to a higher being, every struggle has its opponent. [Demonstrate all this with music:] Hamlet discusses 'to be or not to be' with himself. Handel's Xerxes sings the famous 'Largo' (though it's actually an aria and a 'larghetto') to his beloved tree. In the case of abstract or imagined addressees, it's best to sing to one of the green emergency exit lights up in the second circle. Leonore's 'Come, hope, do not let the last star of the weary be extinguished' – green light. Figaro's 'Se vuol balllare il signor contino' – no, not to the green light, but to the door instead that leads to the Count's chambers.

When a dog growls at you, it wants to tell you that it will bite if you don't go away. The crocodile doesn't even engage in such a discussion, but just swallows the addressee. Once again: there is no expression without an addressee. There is just one sad exception to this universal rule: bad opera. You can perhaps experience it for yourself the next time you go to the theatre. Or instead, observe in the following aria, sung by Cherubino, how a poetic, general addressee – 'women' – turns into a specific one – the Countess – as he weaves a love story under the guise of a poetry recitation.

[There follows Cherubino's aria 'Voi che sapete' from the second act of *The Marriage of Figaro*.]

The Marriage of Figaro is a work with many doors. Closed doors are obstacles, and obstacles are good because they create expression. In general, people don't want to reveal their inner thoughts and feelings, and try to hide them instead. But an obstacle reveals them and makes them perceptible. [Hampe plays out the following:] If I look out of the door and lean to one side because the doorpost hinders my view, then this intensifies my expression and increases the interest of the object outside that I'm trying to observe. The obstacle – the doorpost – makes me more expressive. Now I want to go out of the door, but a chair is in my way. So I sink down onto it in despair because I've just lost a million. Or I kick it into the corner, furious at the fraudster who's just cheated me of the money. But if the whole thing turns out to be a mistake and I've actually won a million, then I can jump for joy over the chair. Each time, the chair – the obstacle in my way – can prompt me to a greater degree of expression than I would otherwise have shown.

Closely related to this technique of incorporating obstacles is the following rule: the comfortable is the enemy of expression. 'What's this he's telling us?' you might well ask. After all, singers need a certain degree of comfort in order to sing beautifully. And indeed, any discomfort must never trap the diaphragm, for that would hinder the singer from actually singing. I can best show what I mean with the help of Rembrandt. He made several sketches for his picture 'Joseph tells Jacob his dream' [Hampe demonstrates everything]. The first shows Jacob sitting comfortably, with little Benjamin between his knees, and he's listening to Joseph who is standing directly in front of him as he explains his dream. That's all well and good, but Rembrandt wasn't happy with it, for it lacked tension. The second sketch shows Jacob sitting once more, again with Benjamin between his knees, but now Joseph is standing on his right side so that Jacob has to turn away from Benjamin to Joseph. It's less comfortable, but clearly more intense. Yet even this did not satisfy Rembrandt. In his third sketch he placed little Benjamin on the other side so that Jacob now has to twist right around to be able to listen to Joseph. This makes Jacob very expressive, and it makes what Joseph is saying much more interesting – because you wouldn't accept such discomfort if what he said wasn't of such importance.

So in the next scene from the second act of *The Marriage of Figaro*, the locked door is the obstacle that ignites expression and leads to a furious marital squabble.

[There follow the trio 'Susanna, or via sortite' and the duettino 'Aprite, presto aprite' from the second act of *The Marriage of Figaro*.]

Incidentally, the little duettino you've just heard can demonstrate how precisely Mozart composed his music for the practical circumstances of staging it. For it allows us to estimate pretty exactly the dimensions of the stage on which the opera was first performed. How come? It's quite simple. Here's the window behind whose curtains Susanna was hiding, and here on the other side we have the locked closet door. When the prelude is played at the right tempo, Susanna will arrive at the door just in time to sing her opening phrase. It can't be more than 12 metres. At the world première, it was exactly 11.5 metres.

And, just as in this example, everything with Mozart demands a quick brain. Often, the poor singers can barely keep up with this play of action and reaction and these lightning-quick changes of expression in the music. With Mozart, you might say: 'Opera is a brain problem.' Keeping 'just ahead' of the music, preparing inwardly for your next phrase and for the next shift in the music – all this is particularly difficult in Mozart. In this regard, those singers who worked with the great conductor Herbert von Karajan were as safe as in the bosom of Abraham, because he always signalled in due time what was coming up next. When we rehearsed together, I wanted to find out how he did it. Eventually I asked him. 'I don't know', he muttered, 'I do my yoga every morning.' I wasn't going to let him off the hook, so I insisted: 'You're conducting one thing, yet inwardly you're already preparing the next. That's almost schizophrenic.' 'No', he answered, 'trizophrenic.' That isn't a word, but he used it anyway. 'Trizophrenic! I give a cue and straightaway I have to signal to the horn: it's too loud. And as I do this, I'm already preparing the next tempo change in advance. You might say: the cue is the present, the horn is already the past and the tempo change is the future.' And indeed, all musicians have to operate on these three levels, especially opera singers. You can't learn it from one day to the next, because it needs a lot of practice. Karajan's 'trizophrenia' creates what I call the 'flow of life' in an operatic performance.

You can experience all of this wonderfully in the finale of the second act.

[There follows the Finale from the
second act of *The Marriage of Figaro*.]
[Pause]

In the first part of this masterclass, you've heard musical numbers and already some recitatives. These recitatives aren't popular with either audiences or performers. They're often shortened, and people try to get over them as quickly as possible. But that's a big mistake! Actually, recitative is a wonderful invention halfway between sung opera and a spoken play. Now: singers are no actors. Nor should they be. They are music-actors. The difference between them is simple to describe. [Hampe demonstrates:] The actor playing Hamlet can speak his monologue slowly and pensively: 'To be or not to be ...'. But he can also laugh out loud, cynically: '... that is the question ...'. In other words, he can make up his own melody. He's free to do that.

Not so music-actors. They are bound to the score as it was written by the composer, and they always have to act within the given musical framework. But in recitatives, they gain something of the freedom of the actor. They are still restricted in their harmony and rhythm, so their acting remains 'musicalized' – as is right and proper for a music-actor. But otherwise, recitatives leave the singers free to determine the tempo, dynamics, accents, pauses and vocal colour that they feel are right for their performance.

Up to now you've heard *secco* recitatives, which are accompanied only by a harpsichord and a bass instrument. They're called 'secco' – 'dry' – because they should not be sung out. Instead, they demand a technique of their own called 'parlare intonato', 'speaking on the tone', which isn't so easy at all. (You can try it yourselves at home in dialogue with your husband or wife!). The next level is 'recitativo accompagnato', namely recitative with orchestral accompaniment. There the singers naturally aren't so free any more, because they have to sing with the orchestra. Nevertheless, they are still far more 'unattached' than in the aria that follows. You can hear all this very nicely in the following aria of the Count at the opening of the third act of *The Marriage of Figaro*. This superb piece will also give you plenty of opportunities to apply your newly acquired abilities as music detectives. One could give a whole masterclass on just this one aria – there is simply so much in it.

[There follow the Count's recitative and aria 'Hai già vinta la causa' from the third act of *The Marriage of Figaro*.]

The Marriage of Figaro, like every great comedy, is really a thwarted tragedy. The essence of comedy lies in the 'lieto fine', the 'happy end'. It gives everyone the feeling: 'Phew! We were lucky, we've been saved by the skin of our teeth!' But what makes something comic in the first place? The characters on stage follow their intentions, they adopt a certain attitude and they fight with each other when necessary. No human being is 'comic' from the outset. Whether or not something is comical is a decision made by you, the audience. Perhaps it arises from an incongruent situation, through unforeseen, contradictory events, through a sudden reversal of fortunes or just someone slipping on a banana skin. Whatever. The comedy doesn't really occur on the stage: it occurs in the auditorium.

You can observe this very clearly in the following scene. Figaro is condemned to pay back a debt to the much older Marcellina this very day, or else he has to marry her. He has no money at all, so he's caught in a trap. He fights for his life like a rat in a cage, defending himself with the most absurd arguments, claiming that he too was born into the nobility and so doesn't even fall under the Count's jurisdiction. His arguments become ever more outrageous. Everyone laughs at him and it all becomes too foolish for the Count, who waves him aside and turns around to leave [demonstrate this]. In the very last second, Figaro cries out 'E sopra tutto' – 'And above all, I have this mark on my arm.' Marcellina: 'In the shape of a spade? On your right arm?' Figaro: 'How do you know that?' Marcellina: 'Oh heavens, it's him ... Raffaello!' It's her own son, abandoned as a baby. Yes, this is funny. But what would have happened if the Count had left just one second earlier, and Figaro hadn't been able to mention the mark on his arm? Where would we have been then? We would have found ourselves in *King Oedipus* by Sophocles, the ancient tragedy at the very dawn of European theatre in which the son marries his mother and sires his own siblings. One second! That's how close comedy and tragedy are to each other. Like all great dramatists, Mozart knew that the happiness of comedy comes at a price – the dark, daemonic source of tragedy.

[There follow the close of the recitative and the sextet from the third act of *The Marriage of Figaro*.]

Do you recall the rather stubborn, masculine theme of Figaro and the charming, feminine oboe of Susanna right at the beginning of the opera? *The Marriage of Figaro* is an opera about men and women – or, more accurately, about women and men. Because women prove to be far superior. For two and a half acts the men engage in intrigue – Figaro, the Count, Basilio and Bartolo – and everything goes awry. Only after the women take matters into their hands does everything turn out well in the end. The turning point is a great aria for the Countess, a genuine miracle of musical psychology – in fact, it's really physiology transformed into music, because the soul can express itself only through the body, through the tension of the breath, the heartbeat, adrenalin and the nerves. The Countess has been abandoned by everyone. The music reflects all her emotions, sometimes with the tiniest harmonic shift of a single note. The hopelessness of her situation becomes clear to her, and you can hear her resignation and despair. But you can also hear how in the end she finds the strength to take her fate into her own hands. No one could do this better than Mozart.

We 'music detectives' are here faced with the task of penetrating to the finest nerve-endings of the music. This is what I call 'micro-management' in music, because the smallest nuance has an impact on the portrayal of her character. At the same time, this portrayal must be infused with the greatest emotional depth and breadth. Where the heart of us normal, healthy human beings registers a temperature of 37 degrees, Mozart sometimes raises it to 370 degrees. How on earth is a poor singer supposed to cope with that? It demands that we pay for it with our own emotions, with our own humanity. 'Pretend' theatre doesn't help here. That's a kind of theatre in which the performer pretends to love or hate but doesn't actually feel anything. The orchestra might sound agitated and the vocal line is at fever pitch of passion – and yet something's missing: the right state of being; the breath of great emotion that alone can make us believe what we see and hear. The singer's body betrays him – his hands above all. His body tells us: 'It's really not so bad, the orchestra doesn't need to get so agitated.' What's lacking is the reality created by his imagination. In opera, sadly, there's a lot of pretending. The path from 'doing' to 'being' is the goal of all theatre. It's a thorny path, and is rarely traversed all the way to its end. Listen now to the aria of the Countess and the recitative that comes before it:

> [There follow the Countess's recitative and aria 'E Susanna non vien ... Dove sono' from the third act of *The Marriage of Figaro*.]

Did you hear the adrenalin? How her heart races, and then at the close how the orchestra with its *sforzato* accents battles and defeats her sense of resignation, carrying her away on a wave of hope?

And now the women take matters into their own hands. They invite the Count to a rendez-vous that evening in the garden, 'Sotto i pini' ['Underneath the pine trees'], which to judge by Susanna's reaction is a spot already known for erotic adventures. The Countess dictates their invitation and Susanna writes it down. It's in the form of a little poem – an improvised quatrain to the evening breeze:

Canzonetta sull'aria
Che soave zeffiretto
Questa sera spirerà
Sotto i pini del boschetto
Dolce amor t'aspetterà.

A little song to the breeze
What a pleasant little zephyr
This evening will sigh
Underneath the pines in the grove;
Sweet love will expect you.

Forgive me – that last line isn't actually sung by the Countess. I made it up. I mentioned earlier that the women are superior. So the Countess does it much more elegantly than I did here, by omitting the final line and instead telling Susanna: 'Ei già il resto capirà' – 'He'll understand the rest' – whatever the precise meaning of 'rest' might be.

Do you remember Mozart's trick with the phrase at the beginning of the overture that was abridged by one measure, from eight to seven, so as to make us feel out of breath? He uses the same trick here, but for a very different purpose. Here he wants to make audible how two women completely understand each other and harmonize despite all social differences, once they share identical interests. You can count on your fingers once again [music]. The voices merge one with the other so that you can barely hear where one stops and the other begins. This little duettino is rightly famous. Nobody could compose women better than Mozart. It couldn't be more feminine.

[There follows the duettino 'Canzonetta sull'aria' from the third act of *The Marriage of Figaro*.]

At the close of the third act, a little revolution takes place. The wedding has gone ahead despite all obstacles, without the Count being able to exercise his feudal, unnatural right to spend the wedding night with the newly married bride – the hated 'Ius primae noctis'. The opera could actually end here. Figaro and Susanna are celebrated as victors by the people. But the real revolution that is at the heart of the opera occurs in the fourth act, at night, out in nature, and outside all societal barriers. If everyone can be united in every imaginable variety of the erotic at every time and in every place – the mighty and lowly, the young and old, the duped and duping – then it becomes obvious how absurd, ridiculous and unnatural are all barriers of social class, regardless of time and place.

But the next tragedy is already lurking amidst the comedy. Figaro has got wind of the invitation to the Count to meet 'sotto i pini'. So he sneaks into the garden after Susanna, actually convinced that she intends to betray him with the Count on their wedding night. Susanna decides in her turn to punish Figaro for his lack of faith and so pretends that she is indeed waiting for her noble lover. And then something happens that could have been composed only by Mozart. Overwhelmed with joy at finally being married to the man she loves, she sings the most wonderful aria of yearning to him – a happy human being, becoming as one with nature, magically transfigured under the starry heavens. And the man she loves is hiding behind the bushes and notices nothing of this at all. Instead, he assumes that she is yearning for the Count. His world falls apart, so that we see and hear on stage the greatest happiness and the deepest unhappiness at one and the same time. Only right at the close of her aria does Susanna notice what she has done, and she whispers a phrase both loving and a bit malicious to her heartbroken husband – who is unable to see or hear anything any more. It includes a word that awakens very different associations if just one of its letters is swallowed: 'IncorOnar di rose' – I want to crown you with roses, you beloved idiot, not, as you think, 'incornar', giving you the 'horns' of the cuckold.

This aria is very, very difficult to sing. The voice has to carry its line just like an instrument, alternating with the woodwinds of the orchestra. The singer mustn't *do* anything here; she just has to *be*. If ever the first and last rule of all theatre were to apply anywhere: then here. It can't be taught, and yet all other rules are nothing without it. It runs: go straight to the heart.

[There follows Susanna's aria 'Deh vieni non tardar' from the fourth act of *The Marriage of Figaro*.]

Poor Figaro is devastated. He mocks himself in his despair. But such desperate self-scorn is dangerous because it could lead to suicide or rampage. Once again we are perilously close to tragedy. And then – with an accent from the orchestra – his gaze falls on you, the audience, so that you and all other blind, stupid men may open your eyes to the true nature of woman. He does this, switching alternately from aggression to sarcasm and screaming pain. These lightning-quick changes in the music are difficult for the singer to realize, not least since he is supposed to be keeping ahead of the orchestra. The danger is that he might descend into a mere rant, which would then make him seem small and ridiculous. In technical terms, he would just be forcing. On the operatic stage, forcing is often mistaken for real intensity [demonstrate]. We frequently see singers jerking forwards and downwards, which can sometimes look like a turkey picking at grains of corn. That is merely forcing; *intensity* is always breath. Big feelings need a big breath, and this is the very opposite of forcing.

There's a rule that can help here – one I learnt from the great baritone Tito Gobbi. 'How you place your feet determines your role'. You can try it out yourself [demonstrate] by imagining a farmer or a sailor walking with a rolling gait – in contrast to the refined leg posture of a prince looking down on the world. Or a slippery sneak like Basilio who's spying on others from just around the corner. Many a tenor who's supposed to be portraying a fiery lover instead straddles the stage as he forces out his notes with his legs wide apart, thus coming across as unintentionally comical.

The singer's feet connect him with the floor and determine his overall posture. This also applies to different attitudes within a role – you see, language itself applies the word 'attitude' here to both physical and emotional states, and ideally we could create a kind of 'body movement score' that might be linked with the musical score. Pay attention to this in Figaro's aria.

Oh, and at the end, there's the matter of the horns in the orchestra. Since you're now experienced music detectives, you'll easily find out what these 'horns' signify.

[There follows Figaro's aria 'Aprite un po' quegl'occhi'
from the fourth act of *The Marriage of Figaro.*]

Now you've passed your final exam brilliantly with the horns. Congratulations! I would like to close by telling you one characteristic of opera that I have not yet mentioned. Something that makes opera irresistible and – I believe – viable for the future. In a sense, it even links it with the most progressive scientific knowledge of our modern times. Because opera can do something that no other art can. Every other art form can only ever show you an excerpt. A painting is by its nature a selection from a much bigger scene. A film is a sequence of images where the camera has to choose. A sculpture can be observed from all sides, but not at the same time. Even the novel, regardless of how swift its mental leaps and associations might be, still takes place in a time sequence.

Music is different, especially opera, because of its concrete nature. Think of a simple two-part canon such as 'Frère Jacques, frère Jacques, dormez-vous?' We hear the first voice and the second, each on his own and yet together at the same time. You can add a third, fourth or fifth voice to the canon to create an ensemble. You will still hear every individual voice, but all of them together too.

In an opera ensemble, you can also add a commentary – perhaps the first voice is lying and the fourth voice is angry about it. But even more: the orchestra could announce that a son with a sword will emerge out of the events on stage. Then you have a leitmotif. And as if that weren't enough, you can also make audible the position of God looking down on His creatures, thus adding His objective perspective to the subjective one of each character. And still you can hear everything on its own, and yet all together at the same time! I know of no other art that can offer such a complete, multi-dimensional image of the world.

This multidimensionality links opera with the most modern scientific perception of our world, which postulates the universe as also being multidimensional. The most recent calculations even propose the existence of countless other universes besides our own, simultaneously emerging and vanishing in many dimensions, so we might actually exist in a multiverse. Opera can do this too, on a small scale. And it does it every day. In its finest moments it can offer us an idea of what exists, barely imaginable, beyond all possibilities of human knowledge.

But let's come back from multiverses and the universe, down to Earth. The finale of the fourth act of *The Marriage of Figaro*, in the park at night-time under the revolving firmament, can give you an idea of all this. The Ancients called it: 'the harmony of the spheres'.

[There follows the finale of the fourth act of *The Marriage of Figaro*.]

Index of names and works